HIERAPOLIS OF PHRYGIA (PAMUKKALE)

AN ARCHAEOLOGICAL GUIDE

YAYINLARI

A. Ceccanti SRL

 Vehbi Koç Vakfı

KÖMÜRCÜOĞLU
MERMER

TURBANITALIA - La Turchia più bella

HIERAPOLIS OF PHRYGIA (PAMUKKALE)

AN ARCHAEOLOGICAL GUIDE

Francesco D'Andria

Italian Archaeological Mission at Hierapolis
English translation by Paul Arthur

The book is published with the contribution of the Italian Ministry of the University
and Scientific and Technological Research (MURST)
Project: Hierapolis of Phrygia. Archaeological excavation and restoration methods.

EGE YAYINLARI

Series "Ancient Cities of Anatolia": 5

Cover picture
Decorative mask from the Ionic capitals (Fig. 87)

English translation
by Paul Arthur

Graphic Design
Savaş Çekiç

Printing
Bilnet Matbaacılık

Production and Distribution
Zero Prodüksiyon
Kitap-Yayın-Dağıtım San. Ltd. Şti.
Abdullah Sokak, No: 17, Taksim
34433 İstanbul
Tel: +90 (212) 244 7521   Fax: +90 (212) 244 3209
e.mail: info@zerobooksonline.com
www.egeyayinlari.com   www.zerobooksonline.com

CONTENTS

"From Asia, rich in its rivers,
you can enjoy the most excellent earth,
Hierapolis, golden city,
Lady of the Nymphs,
adorned with splendid springs"

Epigram from the *diazoma* of the theatre

Visit the Hierapolis homepage at
www.misart.it
with links to other Italian archaeological Missions in Turkey

Preface

The archaeological guide to Hierapolis wants to represent an instrument for the spreading of scientific information for those who visit this important archaeological site in Turkey. The book also constitutes a synthesis of the work that the Italian Archaeological Mission at Hierapolis is involved in, and records the principal results obtained during the course of the excavations and restoration. Work began in 1957, the year in which Paolo Verzone founded the Italian Archaeological Mission. In this centenary year of his birth I give him my gratitude and warmest thoughts. I also wish to thank Daria de Bernardi Ferrero, Tullia Ritti and Paul Arthur, who have read this text, for their useful remarks.

Various events have caused the late publication of this guide. For this reason details of the recent excavations are not included. The podium in travertine (14) can be now interpreted as part of a vast thermal complex probably dating to the Flavian phase of the Roman Period (end of 1st century AD). New extraordinary discoveries have also brought interest to the area where the Sanctuary of Apollo is sited. Furthermore, the preparation of the Museum has undergone some modifications. I have preferred not to further delay the publication of this guide and have decided that any updated news or information will be published in a future edition.

I wish to thank all those who have contributed to the success of the Italian Archaeological Mission at Hierapolis. This includes the workers, students, technicians, conservationists, archaeologists and architects from both Italy and Turkey. A special thanks goes to the Italian Embassy in Ankara, to the Turkish Embassy in Rome, to the officials of the Denizli Museum, to the Ministry of Culture of Turkey, and to Dr. Alpay Pasinli, General Director for Monuments and Museums.

The Mission has always counted on the support of the Italian Universities of Lecce, Genoa, Venice, Catholic-Milan, Frederick II of Naples, and Bari. All have participated in the project and have adhered to CIRDAR, the International Departmental Centre of Research, Documentation and Archaeological Restoration, established at the Polytechnic School of Turin. I wish to express my gratitude to the Rectors of these Universities on behalf of all those who toil so as to get to know, to conserve, and to bring further value to the ancient city of Hierapolis.

HISTORY OF THE CITY

Before the foundation

Rare traces of prehistoric occupation of the plateau (fragments of obsidian).

Development of a cult site around the cave of the Plutonion (see p. 142)

Town of *Kydrara* on the site of the later city of Hierapolis (?).

Third century BC

Control of the region by the Hellenistic kingdom of the Seleucids and probable foundation of the city. The names of the tribes incised on the steps of the theatre indeed refer to the Seleucid dynasty based on the capital at Antioch.

The name Hierapolis signifies "the holy city" because of the religious traditions that developed around the sacred cave.

Cult of Apollo Archegetes, protector of the new Hellenic colonies.

190 BC

Battle of Magnesia: Rome and King Eumenes II of Pergamum, as allies, defeat the Seleucid King Antiochus III.

188 BC

The Peace of Apamea in Syria: Asia Minor, up to the Taurus mountains, is assigned to the Attalid dynasty, and thus Hierapolis becomes part of the kingdom of Pergamum. The city emits a decree in honour of Apollonides, Queen of Pergamum and wife of Attalus I, after his death around 165 BC

133 BC

King Attalus III of Pergamum bequethes his kingdom, including Hierapolis, to Rome.

The city is assigned to the juridical circumscription, which capital was at Cibyra.

From the second century BC to the first century AD

Development of industrial activities, in particular those regarding wool production and the dyeing of textiles.

Strabo (Augustan times) refers to the hot waters which have the property of fixing colours to woollen weaves; a plant (the madder root) produced a red dye, similar to purple but a lot cheaper. In Julio-Claudian times (first half of the first century AD) the *heroon* or so-called "Tomba Bella" (7) was built in honour of a very important person linked to Hierapolis.

AD 60   Under Nero *(Nero Claudius Drusus Germanicus Caesar)* (AD 54-68)

An earthquake destroys the city along with neighbouring Colossae and Laodicea.

AD 86   Under Domitian *(Titus Flavius Domitianus)* (AD 81-96)

Construction of the gates and the "Street of Frontinus" that signals the reconstruction of Hierapolis by the emperors of the Flavian dynasty: Temple of Apollo, theatre, gymnasium?, roads and tombs, including the noteworthy example of the merchant Flavius Zeuxis.

Hadrian *(Traianus Hadrianus Augustus)* (117-138)

Probable visit of the emperor who, as a sign of goodwill, gave back to the city the *aurum coronarium*, a conspicuous sum of money that cities offered to the emperor in celebration of their elevation to the throne. Extraordinary economic development that continues for the whole of the second and the beginning of the third century.

Construction of the monumental Agora complex.

Erection of statues in honour of the emperor and his wife Sabina.

Antoninus Pius *(Aelius Hadrianus Antoninus Augustus)* (138-161)

The city, which housed a substantial Hebrew community, continues to expand its economic activity.

Christianity develops: Papias and Apollinarius are second century bishops.

Marcus Aurelius *(Marcus Aurelius Antoninus)* (161-180)

> Plague breaks out amongst the Roman troops returning from an expedition to the East. Hierapolis turns to the oracle of Apollo at Claros, near Colophon, for advice.

Septimius Severus *(Lucius Septimius Severus Pertinax)* (193-211)

> The city's development continues as the settlement thrives. The most important families continue to erect funerary monuments in the cemeteries during the course of the century.

> Growing prestige of the "ecumenical" games in honour of Apollo Pythios, in which many cities participated, together with the Olympic and Actian games.

> The sophist Antipater, member of an aristocratic family of Hierapolis, gains great influence at the Imperial court as mentor of princes and as chancellor of the Greek-speaking cities.

> Construction of numerous public monuments: amongst the most complex is the *scaenae frons* of the theatre, completed in AD 210-211 under the proconsul Quintus Tineius Sacerdos.

Caracalla *(Marcus Aurelius Antoninus)* (211-217)

> Antipater manifests his disapproval of the murder of Geta by his brother Caracalla, made Emperor. Anger of Caracalla and "suicide" of Antipater. Philostratos, author of the "Lives of the Sophists", defines Hierapolis as one of the most prosperous cities of Asia Minor.

Elagabalus *(Varius Avitus Bassianus)* (218-222)

> The much sought after title *neokoros*, "custodian of the temple" for the Imperial cult, is assigned to Hierapolis.

Alexander Severus *(M. Aurelius Severus Alexander)* (222-235)

> Construction of the large Nymphaeum of the Tritons (12) at the northern entrance to the city.

AD 352

> Restorations of the *scaenae frons* of the theatre attested by inscriptions.

Second half of the fourth century AD

Erection of a statue to the Praetorian Prefect of the Orient, Strategius Musonianus (after AD 360), hailed as benefactor of the city.

An earthquake seriously damages the monuments. Inscriptions attest to new restorations to the theatre. The Agora complex is not restored and is gradually destroyed.

Theodosius *(Flavius Theodosius)* (379-395)

Construction of the defensive wall circuit around the city, with two main gates, to the north and to the south, that leaves out large areas such as the Agora.

Fifth-sixth century AD

Transformation of Hierapolis into a Christian city. Prestige due to the presence of the tomb of Philip the Apostle, like St. John at Ephesus. At the beginning of the fifth century the Apocryphal Acts of Philip are written, naming Hierapolis *Ophiorhyme*, "city of the serpents", in relation to the viper cult, which the Apostle would have abolished by converting the inhabitants to Christianity.

Abandonment of buildings such as the theatre and construction of churches, including the Cathedral, the *Martyrion* of St. Philip, the Pier Church and the suburban church (Baths-Basilica). The Plutonium is still a place to visit. In the time of Justinian some writers, such as Damascius, claim to have entered the cave through inspiration of the goddess Cybele.

AD 535   Hierapolis becomes metropolis of *Phrygia Pacatiana secunda.*

First half of the seventh century AD Heraclius ? (610-641)

A new ruinous earthquake seriously damages the city and leaves the most important monuments in ruin.

Eighth to tenth century AD

Ruralization of the city with the construction of houses above the ruins and small chapels on the sites of the ancient churches.

	Presence of bishops attested in the Acts of the Church Councils.
1190	The crusade of Frederick Barbarossa passes through the ruined city "where it is said that the Apostle Philip is buried".

Eleventh to thirteenth century

Construction of the castle on the western edge of the plateau.

Use of the Roman baths as a prestige residence.

Thirteenth century

The Seljuk Turks control the territory.

Hierapolis is abandoned. In the plain of the Lykos river the caravanserai of Akhan is built, employing classical marbles from Laodicea.

Foundation of the Emirate of Denizli.

Magistracies and public functions attested in the inscriptions from Hierapolis (from Tullia Ritti):

The population was divided into fifteen tribes, whose names are inscribed on the steps of the theatre. The following are easy to read: Apolloniàs, Tiberianè, Rhomaìs, Eumenìs, Seleukìs, Laodikìs, Attalìs, Stratonikìs and Antiochìs.

The city was governed by the Boulè (Council) and the Demos (Popular assembly). The inscriptions attest priestly functions in honour of Apollo, Aphrodite Urania, Demetra, Dionysos, Gerusìa, Boulè, and the high priest (archiereus) of the cult of the emperors.

Agonothetes: organiser of games.

Archiereus: priest of the tributary cult of the Emperors.

Agoranomos: Inspector of markets.

Boulè: Council. Initially elective though later, in Imperial times, formed by the ruling class with effective political and administrative power.

Demos: Popular assembly with the formal power to ratify decisions taken by the Boulè.

Gerusìa: Association of city elders selected because of their wealth and prestige.

Koinon: Association of the Greeks of Asia, presided over by a leading citizen, that held its assembly once a year in the major cities, by rotation.

Neoi: Association of youths selected for their wealth and prestige.

Paraphylax: Guard responsible for controlling the territory.

Stephanephoros: Bearer of the crown in public ceremonies. An annual investiture that brought with it the responsibility of handing out sometimes money to the public administration. It also brought the privilege of giving one's own name to the year.

Strategos: Magistrate of the civil administration that, despite its name, held no military power.

HISTORY OF RESEARCH AND EXCAVATIONS

1678-1699   The first descriptions of the city by travellers such as J. Spon, G. Wheler and T. Smith, that refer to the vast necropolis and the white travertine cascades.

1745   As well as the necropolis, R. Pococke describes other monuments, including the theatre; he identifies the nymphaeum as the Temple of Apollo.

1775   R. Chandler, with the contribution of the English Society of Dilettanti, visits Hierapolis and reads various inscriptions of the theatre.

1812   C. R. Cockerell describes the Plutonium.

1828   V. J. Arundel also documents the presence of the sacred grotto.

1838   L. De Laborde describes the site and its monuments.

1839   C. Fellows interprets the ruins of the baths as a palace.

    Ch. Texier illustrates the principle monuments.

1858   Ch. Trémaux draws a plan of the city and reconstructions of the theatre.

Second half of the nineteenth century   The descriptions of travellers increase: E. J. Davis (1874), A. Choisy (1876 and 1883), W. M. Ramsey (1882-1897).

1898   The first comprehensive description of the city appears in a volume by C. Humann, C. Cichorius, W. Judeich and F. Winter, presenting topographical, architectural and artistic aspects, devoting space to the necropolis and the first major collection of inscriptions.

1957	Beginning of systematic research and restoration by the Italian Archaeological Mission founded by Paolo Verzone, supported by the great Turkish archaeologist Arif Müfid Mansel. Official Italian research in Anatolia, which had been suspended in 1939 at Aphrodisias, recommenced thanks to Prof. Verzone, who was temporarily in Turkey as Professor of the History of Architecture at the Teknik Universitesi of Istanbul.
1957-1969	Study by the Italian Archaeological Mission of the urban plan and Christian monuments. Excavation of the *martyrion* of St. Philip and the Temple of Apollo. Restoration of the Frontinus Gate and of some of the funerary monuments in the necropolis. Beginning of work at the theatre with the contribution, in 1960-61, of the General Directorate of Antiquities and Museums of Turkey.
1970-1971	Systematic investigation of the street pattern and identification of the orthogonal layout of the city, with elongated insulae.
1972-1979	Excavations of the theatre begin again. Restoration of the proscaenium. From 1978 the direction is under Daria De Bernardi Ferrero, of Turin Polytechnic, with the scientific responsibility of Paolo Verzone with regard to the Turkish government.
1980-1983	Museum constructed within the Roman baths. Restoration at the theatre, particularly regarding the podium of the stage or *scaenae frons*. Beginning of work in the vast northern area to the east of the Street of Frontinus. Identification of the Agora, surrounded by colonnaded Ionic porticoes in marble.
1984-1989	Restoration of various buildings in the necropolis. Total excavation of the Street of Frontinus, with removal of thick calcareous deposits. Great development in mass tourism, that includes Hierapolis amongst its objectives, also because of the attraction of the travertine cascades. The Association of Friends of Hierapolis is constituted in 1987. In 1988

	Hierapolis-Pamukkale is included in the UNESCO World Heritage List of the convention concerning the protection of World Cultural and Natural Heritage (List no. 485).
1989	Beginning of systematic excavation of a block to the north of the theatre and of the study of the houses of Hierapolis.
1990-1991	Organisation of the area of the Agora and of the Gate and Street of Frontinus. Restoration of some tombs of the northern necropolis, with the help of sponsors (Mrs. Helga Winkler - Fowa Turin).
1992-2000	Important restorations to the theatre and of part of the cemeteries, with contributions by Fiat of Istanbul and the Koç Foundation. The General Directorate of Antiquities and Turkish Museums begins a programme of conservation of the natural environment and travertine formations, as well as restoring part of the baths and the southern area of the city. Two entrances to the site, with facilities to cope with the large number of tourists, are built to the north and south of the city. Research and excavations of the medieval castle begin in 1994.

The team of the Italian Archaeological Mission is formed of architects, archaeologists, students and technicians of the Turin Polytechnic and the Universities of Lecce, Naples, Milan (Catholic University), Venice.

Research and excavation is financed by the Italian Ministry of Foreign Affairs, the Ministry of Universities and Scientific and Technological research, the Ministry of Cultural Heritage, the National Research Council, the Turin Polytechnic, the University of Lecce, as well as by private sponsors including Fowa of Turin and FIAT of Istanbul, together with the Koç Foundation, A. Ceccanti SRL, Turban Italia, ENI.

THE SITE
GEOGRAPHICAL BACKGROUND

Hierapolis lies in the *Vilayet* (Province) of the modern city of Denizli. It is located on a plateau characterised by the presence of spectacular thermal phenomena that overlooks the large valley of the river Çürüksu (the ancient Lykos), one of the tributaries of the Maeander. The eastern part of the city extends along the slopes of hills that form the edge of the central-western Anatolian plateau.

The plain of the Lykos is dominated by two massif mountains. The volcano of Honaz Dağ (ancient *Kadmos*), rises 2751 metres high to the south-east, whilst the picturesque wooded Baba Dağ (ancient mount *Salbakos*) rises to the south, separating the Lykos valley from the Tavas (Tabai) plateau and the plain of Aphrodisias.

The area lies at the junction of ancient routes that, through river valleys and mountain passages, connect it to various regions. Thus it may be considered a transit area between the internal Anatolian plateau and the Aegean world. Indeed, in antiquity, the area was crossed by a secondary route of the Royal road that linked Persia with the Mediterranean.

The bountiful Lykos valley is well watered and today is used mainly for the cultivation of cotton, though numerous vineyards on the hills yield the very sweet grapes of Smyrna. Through the Maeander and the city of Aydın (ancient *Tralles*) it is linked to the Aegean coastlands. Passing through a mountain passage and the

Fig. 1 Satellite image of the Lykos valley (by kind permission of Telespazio).

Fig. 3 Laodicea on the Lykos. Aerial view with the two theatres.

city of Alaşehir (ancient *Philadelphia*) one reaches the neighbouring *Hermos* valley, where the ancient cities of *Sardis* and *Magnesia*
are located, and from there can reach the coast at Smyrna. To the
east it is connected to the region of the Eğridir lakes and through
Pisidia to the Pamphylian coast and the city of Antalya (the
ancient Hellenistic centre of *Attaleia*).

Such a favourable position for agriculture and commerce
led the Lykos valley in antiquity to become a basin of intense
demographic expansion, where numerous cities and myriad

Fig. 2 Map of Asia Minor showing the main centres (O. Henry).

Fig. 4   Laodicea on the Lykos. Aerial view with the theatre.

villages were born and flourished. *Colossae*, the most ancient of
the cities in the area, cited by Herodotus, grew up at the foot of
Mount Kadmos. The Seleucid foundation of *Laodicea* developed
in front of Hierapolis, to retain the economic and administrative
primacy of the area. The city of *Tripolis*, with conspicuous archaeological remains, appeared at the confluence of the Lykos and
Maeander. Last but not least, the city of *Trapezopolis*, less wealthy
and with fewer large buildings, developed in the wooded land of
Mount *Salbakos*.

Fig. 5 Karahayıt: the red springs.

Fig. 6 Tripolis on the Maeander: the grape harvest.

The Lykos formed a frontier zone, and for this reason ancient geographers are not in agreement in siting Hierapolis in Lydia, Phrygia or Caria. During the centuries, Phrygia seems to be the preferred area for Hierapolis, bordering Caria, in which, according to the geographer Ptolemy, *Laodicea* and *Tripolis* would be placed. The original religious character of Hierapolis (the sacred city) was gradually enriched with the addition to its territory of the village of *Thiounta* (modern Gözler), rich in marble quarries, near to which lay the sanctuary of Apollo Kareios. Even further to the east, lying some forty kilometres away, was the sanctuary of Lairbenos, another native deity assimilated to Apollo, with the town of *Motella*, strongly linked to Hierapolis.

Fig. 7
Karahayıt: women at the springs.

THE TRAVERTINE CASCADES

The ruins of Hierapolis lie in a locality called Pamukkale, a Turkish word meaning "castle of Cotton", because of the travertine foundations which, due to their morphological variety and extraordinary whiteness, recall the flowers of that plant.

Fig. 8
Calcareous
concretions
at Pamukkale.

Fig. 9 Channels dividing the fields in the plain of Pamukkale.

Fig. 10 The travertine basins.

These deposits form continuously with the abundant flow of water, at 250 litres a second, that gushes from local thermal springs at a temperature of 35°. The reduction of pressure creates a carbon dioxide loss, thus depositing calcium carbonate in a thin layer that grows some 3 cm per annum! In this way the immense banks of travertine that characterise the site's morphology have been created, resulting in a landscape of inimitable fascination.

The most varied and fantastic cascades have formed on the edge of the plateau, whilst in the valley the water has created solidified channels that cross the fields and are still used today for irrigation and land boundaries, just as Vitruvius described them in Augustan times (*De architectura*, VIII, 3):

"In the same way, at Hierapolis in Phrygia, a large quantity of hot water gushes forth, from which derivations are created by excavating ditches around gardens and vineyards; after a year this

Fig. 11 The travertine basins in winter.

29

becomes a rock crust. Then every year, by building earthen borders to the left and to the right, they make the water pass internally so as to obtain, through this crust, divisions for their fields".

If, along the edge of the plateau, spectacular cascades are formed which have attracted millions of tourists, on the plateau the limestone has accumulated in layers of great thickness that cover the ancient ruins.

All the area below the spring-line is now covered by a layer of stratified stone, sometimes reaching a depth of up to four metres, that seals buildings, sculptures, objects and all that went to create the urban site of Hierapolis. This creates a difficult problem for archaeologists who need to resort to the use of pneumatic drills to break-up the hard calcareous deposit, especially along the main north-south street *(plateia)* where, in the middle ages, the waters found a natural course down which to flow.

Fig. 12 View of the travertine basins (from De Laborde, 1838).

In the area around the Pamukkale Hotel, corresponding to the centre of the ancient city, a small lake was formed to host the spring water, submerging the remains of a marble portico with its collapsed fluted columns and creating an extraordinary effect of natural and cultural harmony. Today, a small concrete wall harnesses the waters, transforming the lake into a pool which is literally invaded by tourists.

So as to safeguard the extraordinary natural balance of the site and territory of Hierapolis, which is seriously threatened by the growth of mass tourism, the General Directorate of Antiquities of Turkey has promoted an ambitious project that offers an incomparable fusion of ancient monuments and natural phenomena. Hierapolis has also been listed by UNESCO as a protected site of world-wide significance (List no. 485).

Fig. 13 Excavation of the calcareous concretions with a pneumatic compressor.

31

Minerals found in solution in a litre of water at the springs of Hierapolis

Cations		Milligrams
Sodium	Na +	5.014
Calcium	Ca ++	446.000
Magnesium	Mg + +	106.140
Iron	Fe +++	scarce
Aluminium	Al +++	"
Anions		
Bicarbonates	HCO_3-	1055.300
Sulphates	SO_4--	651.024
Chlorides	Cl-	17.750
Nitrates	NO_3-	-
Nitrites	NO_2-	-
Metasilicate acids	H_2SiO_3	350.700
Total		2331.928

In a litre of water there are about 2.5 grams of minerals in solution.

Analysis conducted by Mehmet Akşehirli on 14th July 1966 (from *Pamukkale National Park, Master Plan for Protection and Use,* 1969).

THE CITY, URBAN LAYOUT

The original nucleus of the settlement, which was clearly the attraction of the population of the Lykos valley prior to the foundation of Hierapolis, is the thermal spring and the sacred cave of the Plutonium. Unfortunately, at the moment, there is no documentation regarding the original religious activity in this area. The city appears in the third century BC, probably as a Seleucid foundation and, following the peace of *Apamea* (188 BC), passes to the reign of *Pergamum* to play a strategic role along the antique frontier between the Pergamum and Seleucid territories, facing the rival *Laodicea*.

Fig. 14 View of the ruins and the Lykos valley from the theatre.

Fig. 15   The small lake prior to the construction of the Pamukkale Hotel (photo by Kachler in 1958).

The urban layout of Hellenistic conception occupies the plateau formed of calcareous spring deposits and extends along the slopes of the backing hills. It is characterised by a Hippodamean-type plan that superimposed an orthogonal network of streets upon the uneven topography. The narrowest streets *(stenopoi)*, three metres wide (about 10 Greek feet), delimit rather long blocks or *insulae*, of about 35 x 70 metres (100 x 250 Greek feet), that are aligned along a principal north-south axis, the *plateia*, which is 14 metres wide. The early public buildings and private houses, which have not yet been found, were located within the primitive Hellenistic foundation.

There are no traces of fortifications, though in this period a watchtower and the steep slopes covered with calcareous formations on the western side of the site will have been enough to guarantee a defence to the city. A natural protection along its southern side was given by a deep channel cut by the *Chrysorhoas* torrent (of the golden waters).

Between the second and first centuries BC the first burials of the necropolis, that was to develop in Imperial times, appeared along the road to the north, that dropped towards *Tripolis* and the Maeander. These included simple graves excavated in the rock and, probably, the first monumental tumulus tombs or barrows, some of which, indeed, have yielded Hellenistic pottery.

We know very little about the early Imperial period, though it includes the *heroon*, erected in the cemetery area to the north of the settlement, and ceramics found in the earth removed during the construction of later tombs, as well as in the backfill of their foundations.

Nonetheless, the original layout survived the devastation created by the Neronian earthquake of AD 60. The monumental structure of the city that we know best is that created during the intense programme of reconstruction that followed the earthquake. This was undertaken with the patronage of the Flavian emperors, of Hadrian, of Antoninus Pius, up to Septimius Severus, in a contin-uous development from the end of the first to the third century AD. Immediately after the earthquake the north-south street axis was enlarged. Stretching for about a kilometre and 350 metres, the original road was added to by another stretch to the north, some 14 metres wide and 170 metres long, flanked by houses and shops. In the southern part of the city a similar stretch of road was added for some 150 metres, also characterised by a Doric façade to the flanking travertine-built buildings. Under the emperor Domitian, the proconsul Julius Frontinus erected two honorary gates with three arched entrances flanked by towers at the two extremities of the road, as a monumental testimony to the civic prestige vis-ible to all who travelled to Hierapolis.

In the same period a programme of reorganisation of the vast area to the east of the *plateia* was underway. It consisted of the levelling of the area with large quantities of fill so as to form the immense square of the Agora (8). During the course of the second century, the area was enriched with the erection of Ionic *stoai*, thus also creating a space which could function for games and gladiatorial combat, and perhaps at the same time the urban area was further enlarged with the construction of baths, close to the northern necropolis.

Monuments were erected in the centre of the settlement, comprising the theatre, the large enclosure of the sanctuary of Apollo, the civic Agora, the gymnasium and, perhaps, also the building of the original nucleus of the central baths. An extended drainage system ran beneath the road. It consisted of channels, covered by travertine blocks, which drained into the large *cloaca* beneath the *plateia*, so as to conduct the waters out of the settlement and into the valley below. On the summit of the eastern hill, a large reservoir (the *castellum aquae*) collected drinking water which, through a capillary system of clay pipes of varying dimensions, was distributed to the public buildings, to the *nymphaea* and to private houses. Under some of the roads many pipes are to be found one above the other, lying only a few centimetres below the ground surface, which was formed of pressed earth to the sides of the road paving.

During the second and third centuries AD, corresponding to the period of economic and commercial development of the city, all the monumental areas were enlarged and enriched with sumptuous marble decoration, statue groups and smaller buildings. Furthermore, the city was furnished with at least two large public *nymphaea*, the Temple Nymphaeum and the Nymphaeum of the Tritons, the latter near the northern entrance to the city, so as to satisfy the needs of caravans.

Fig. 16 View of the archaeological site (from De Laborde, 1838).

The cemeteries developed particularly along the north access road to the city, though also along the southern one. They were an immediate reflection of the complex social life of the community of Hierapolis, with their varied typology of funerary monuments inspired, through their rich decoration, by the idea of the heroon, with a base *(bomòs)* upon which were set the travertine or marble sarcophagi of the principal members of the family. More modest tombs, with chambers placed in parallel rows giving the impression of rock-cut burials, were located along the eastern slopes.

This large-scale urban development which, through recent excavations we are beginning to get to know even as far as domestic architecture is concerned, with the discovery of the sumptuous "House of the Ionic columns" around a central peristyle, came to an abrupt end during the course of the fourth century AD. Following a violent earthquake in the latter half of the century, large areas of the city, such as the Agora, were abandoned to spoliation and eventually destroyed. The city attempted to refortify itself by the building of a fortification, set up between the late fourth and the early fifth century, following imperial legislation of AD 395 by Theodosius, that obliged cities to defend themselves with walls against barbarian invasions.

The fortifications, though erected with the reuse of stone blocks, and thus not displaying the regularity in construction of earlier Imperial buildings, nonetheless create an imposing structure. It possesses two gates flanked by square towers placed at the two main, north and south, entrances to the city, as well as two postern gates that connect the settlement to the *Martyrion* of St. Philip and to the eastern necropolis. It has 24 square towers, set at varying distances from each other, obviously positioned for strategic reasons so as to control the surrounding territory. Radical transformations of the city begin in the fifth and sixth centuries, with a process of deterioration of the ancient urban layout. The area of the Agora was neglected and transformed into a chaotic industrial area for the production of bricks, tiles and everyday ceramics, with large dumps of pottery wasters left abandoned right in the centre of the ancient piazza. This is, however, also a sign of a certain amount of building work still taking place within the settlement. The shops along the "Street of Frontinus" are transformed into houses that make use of reworked and fragmented stone from ancient monuments. The houses also occupy part of the street, thus halving its width and destroying its original monumental aspect. These transformations may be seen throughout the city: the theatre, which had been restored during the fourth century, was no longer used for theatrical representations. Its

Fig. 17 Landscape with badlands around the Lykos valley.

original architectural forms were altered as it was invaded by houses, and a bread oven was even constructed behind the stage!

Alongside the decline of the classical buildings, new monumental poles are provided by the appearance of churches that reflect a high level of architectural culture, in which local building traditions were renewed under impulses from Constantinople. Hierapolis also becomes an important centre of Christianity through the cult centred on the tomb of Philip the Apostle, and, in 535, the city is elevated to metropolis of *Phrygia Pacatiana secunda.* The suburban church (the Baths-Basilica), the Cathedral with its baptistery and the Church with Piers are aligned along the main street, whilst the architectural masterpiece of the *Martyrion* of St. Philip rises on the eastern hill.

The churches of Hierapolis provide splendour to the late antique Christian city, in which religious buildings overshadow an urban layout frequently subject to chaotic transformations, reflecting serious social contrasts. This is the city that is annulled by a violent earthquake that, through archaeology, has been dated to the first half of the seventh century. The most recent coins

Fig. 18   View of the ancient city and the calcareous formations.

discovered within the collapsed masonry date to the reign of Heraclius, though many belong to the emperors Justinian and Justin II, indicating intense activity during the course of the sixth century. The earthquakes lead to the collapse of the Theodosian walls, the theatre, the churches, and such Roman monuments as were still standing, such as the Nymphaeum of the Tritons which had been enveloped by the Byzantine fortifications. By this time there are no longer the resources, financial or human, to reconstruct the city and the survivors reorganise the settlement in a new fashion: the houses, poor and without pretensions, are built upon the remains of the earlier buildings, recovering building material from the ruins. It is a long process that lasts up to the thirteenth century. The regular urban layout of the classical city appears totally cancelled and the houses are erected over the ancient streets, whilst tortuous paths link the various settlement nuclei, leaving large areas free to be cultivated or to be used for grazing. Small churches are erected within the shells of the large proto-Byzantine churches. In this progressive process of ruralisation, points of reference are represented by the Castle, which rises in a strategic position on an outcrop of the plateau overlooking the valley, and the Baths, which at this time seem to provide the residence for those who appear to hold positions of power.

Finally, from the thirteenth century, the settlement system of the new inhabitants, the Seljuk Turks, leads to the abandonment of what is left of the city, and life shifts down to the Lykos valley, where the caravanserai of Akhan exemplifies the new historical and cultural reality that now dominates the region.

The ruins of Hierapolis host the poor houses of peasants and shepherds and the tombs, profaned and emptied by treasure hunters, serve as refuges for brigands.

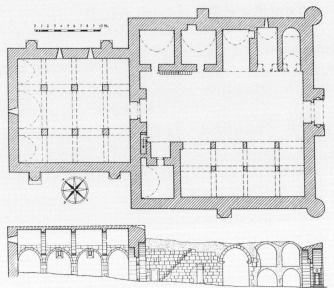

Fig. 19
Plan and section of the caravanserai of Akhan.

Fig. 20
Portal of Akhan.

ITINERARY (see plan)

The plateau upon which lie the imposing ruins of Hierapolis may be reached from the village of Pamukkale (once Ecirli köy), by either one of two recently built roads that lead respectively to the northern and southern entrances of the ancient city. An ambitious project by the Turkish government has permitted the recent creation of two reception areas for tourists visiting both the archaeological area and the nature park, the latter composed of the travertine cascades and thermal springs.

Leaving the village of Pamukkale, the road to the northern gate rises along a tortuous route that allows one to see, up on the left, the ruins of Hierapolis above the plateau from which descend the old channels which now form high travertine barriers. The channels form an imposing natural spectacle that took centuries to build up, and which nature itself has partly demolished through repeated earthquakes. This unique landscape of creation and demolition helps to prepare us for the vision of the ruins of the ancient city, further devastated by seismic activity through the centuries. In the first century BC, Strabo (Geography, XII, 8) wrote: "I might almost say that the whole of the territory in the neighbourhood of the Maeander is subject to earthquakes and is undermined with both fire and water as far as the interior; for, beginning at the plains, all these conditions extend through that country to the Charonia [the caves, like the Plutonium, considered to be entrances to Hades], I mean the Charonium at Hierapolis and that at Acharaca in Nysais and that near Magnesia and Myous. In fact, the soil is not only friable and crumbly but is also full of salts and easy to burn out"(translation by H.L. Jones, Loeb Ed.). Similar phenomena took place in the neighbouring region of Philadelphia in Lydia, which the ancients called Katakekaumene or the soil that burns.

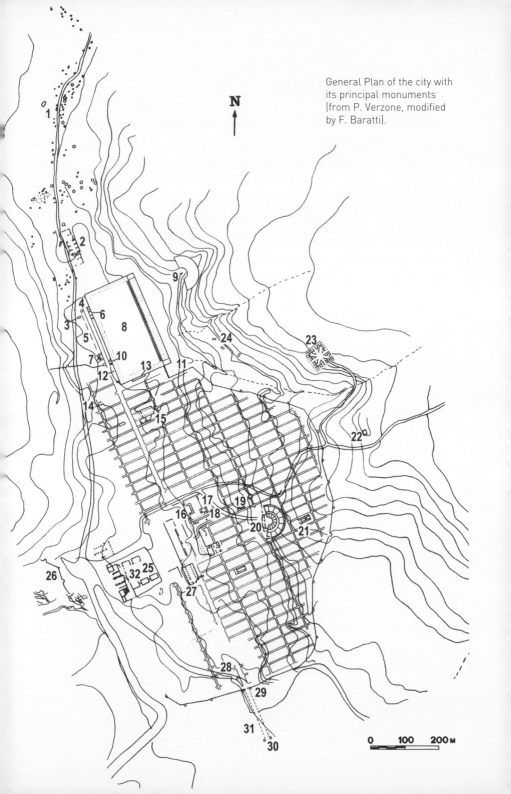

General Plan of the city with
its principal monuments
(from P. Verzone, modified
by F. Baratti).

N

0   100   200 M

Having reached the plateau, the ancient road is recognisable for the presence of the evermore frequent ancient funerary monuments. To the right, amongst the thick vegetation, it is possible to see a travertine base, upon which still sits a marble sarcophagus decorated with garlands.

The building complex of the recently constructed tourist centre marks the beginning of the itinerary; an imposing roof of glass domes sits upon metal piers which, with its modern linear design and materials, contrasts quite singularly with the surrounding arid landscape with its warm tones of brown and yellow of the travertine mountain.

The itinerary which we propose will allow a visit to the ancient city following the route of ancient travellers who reached the Aegean coast along the road that ran down the Maeander valley. Having arrived at Tripolis, they entered the Lykos valley by climbing up the plateau of Hierapolis; here the road meets the first funerary buildings and thus enters the **Northern Necropolis (1)**

ITINERARY
Northern entrance from Karahayıt and the valley of the Maeander

1) Northern Necropolis
2) Baths-Basilica
3) Tomb of Flavius Zeuxis and other funerary buildings
4) Frontinus Gate
5) Frontinus Street
6) Latrine
7) "Tomba Bella"
8) Agora
9) Suburban Theatre
10) North Byzantine Gate
11) Byzantine Walls
12) Nymphaeum of the Tritons

13) Byzantine Baths
14) Travertine Podium
15) Cathedral Church
16) Temple Nymphaeum
17) Temple of Apollo
18) Plutonium
19) House of the Ionic Capitals
20) Theatre
21) Church above the Theatre
22) Castellum Aquae (public reservoir)
23) Octagonal Martyrion of St. Philip

24) Eastern Necropolis
25) Large Baths
26) Medieval Castle
27) Pier Church
28) Gymnasium
29) South Byzantine Gate
30) South Frontinus Gate (?)
31) Southern Necropolis
32) Archaeological Museum

Visualization of
Hierapolis in the 3rd c.
(J. Cl. Golvin, 1998).

Northern Necropolis [1]

The visit to the necropolis is quite an experience given the extraordinary state of conservation of the monuments and the vastness of the area in which the funerary buildings are mixed with numerous travertine sarcophagi (more than two thousand have been recorded, many of which bear inscriptions in which they are indicated with the term *soròs*).

Fig. 21   Aerial view of the northern necropolis with sarcophagi, funerary buildings and barrows or tumuli.

The funerary architecture at Hierapolis breaks down into an exceptional variety of types and solutions. The oldest sepulchres are certainly those of tumulus or barrow shape, dating to Hellenistic times (second to first century BC), in which the vaulted funerary chamber is covered by an artificial earth dome surrounded by a cylindrical drum formed of squared blocks. A *dromos* or corridor gives access to the funerary chamber. Usually the tumuli were surmounted by a stone marker in the shape of a phallus so as to protect them from evil influences. The tumuli line the road and rise up the eastern slope overlooking the city.

If these monuments were reserved for eminent families, simple tombs and rock-cut graves served to house the bodies of the poor. The other funerary monuments, which during the first, and

Fig. 22 Balloon view of the northern necropolis.

Fig. 23 Balloon view of the barrows or tumuli of the northern necropolis.

Fig. 24 Balloon view of a barrow or tumulus and sarcophagi in the northern necropolis.

particularly the second and third centuries, occupied the whole area to the north of the city, were usually surrounded by small enclosures which contained gardens with flowers and trees, often cypresses.

The buildings, all in travertine, display a great diversity of types: from the simple sarcophagus placed upon a base, which at times takes the form of a building with a room and funerary beds, to the mortuary chapel with a gabled roof, or with a flat roof upon which one or more sarcophagi were placed, to even more complex buildings with façades that imitated those of the city houses. The base upon which the sarcophagi were placed is indicated in inscriptions with the Greek term *bomòs* (pedestal, altar), and has a precise symbolic significance: by placing the body of the

Fig. 25 The buildings of the northern necropolis along the road. In the centre is Tomb no. A.174.

deceased up high, his memory was exalted. In this way these monuments play the same role as the *heroa* (sepulchres reserved for heroes and great historical figures, for which they celebrate the apotheosis).

The sarcophagi and buildings preserve a very rich series of inscriptions that usually bear the names of the owners of the sepulchre and the indication of the fines to be paid by whosoever should damage them, with the obligation to register such rules in the public archives. The fines were to be paid to the imperial treasury, to the Boulè, to the Gerusia, to the professional associations or to the religious confraternities which also guaranteed the performance of rites in honour of the deceased and the periodic deposition of crowns on the tombs.

The tour begins at the northern entrance, along the ancient road recently brought to light by the Italo-Turkish excavations. The road, eight metres wide and paved with river cobbles, is flanked by sarcophagi, some of which are placed on a base characterised by a large extending cornice with a straight profile. Along the edges of the street are some marble sarcophagus lids. Grain fields with travertine channels acting as boundaries, just as in the description of Vitruvius, may be seen extending away from the tombs, towards the valley.

To the left is a complex of buildings, recently restored by the Italian Archaeological Mission, within stone enclosures in which may be seen the *bomòs* that contains the funerary beds. It may be noted that the doors of the funerary chapels do not open onto the road, but rather to the inside of the enclosure, clearly functioning for the commemorative reunions for the dead in which members of the family would be present.

At the point at which the road starts to rise, in front of the recently restored tomb 175, there stands a funerary chapel (no. 176)

Fig. 26 Tomb no. 114 of Aelius Apollinarius.

Fig. 27 Tomb no. 56.

characterised by a singular façade. The entrance, with two door jambs, a moulded architrave and a series of windows divided by semi-columns, recalls the façades of houses at Hierapolis. Inside are a pair of travertine sarcophagi, whilst two small vaulted features, perhaps intended to contain ossuaries, are visible on the back wall.

After a pause so as to enjoy the picturesque layout of the tombs that extend towards the city, the itinerary continues towards tomb 175, characterised by a very low entrance and, within, by a double row of beds formed of large monolithic blocks. In the centre of another enclosure is a marble sarcophagus with garlands, only partially worked, having arrived directly from the quarry without having been completed on the spot.

An attractive travertine sarcophagus with a Greek inscription lies against tomb 174 (fig. 25). From here one enters an enclosure containing a chapel and a base with a marble sarcophagus decorated with fluting and the head of a satyr, and another in travertine with a well preserved inscription, decorated with reliefs showing two birds pecking at a bunch of grapes and an ear of millet.

Fig. 28 Funerary stele of a gladiator found in the northern necropolis.

Further along are the remains of another marble sarcophagus with a lid upon which is represented a couple, lying down as though participating in a banquet.

To the right hand side of the road is tomb 170, with its elegant moulded base. On its façade is a marble plaque flanked by volutes, which contained the now abraded inscription.

The road continues straight. To the right the tombs are built with vaulted substructures so as to overcome the slope towards the valley. Where the road turns to the right is tomb 162, composed of two adjoining buildings. A partially worked marble sarcophagus with garlands and an inscription rests against the rear wall of the first building. The inscription, datable to the second or third century AD, cites Marcus Aurelius Ammianus Menandrianus and indicates the fine of 1.500 denari to be paid by whoever takes illegal possession of the sepulchre. On the other, travertine, sarcophagus, to the right, is the name of Aelia Glykonis and the usual formula that records the amount of the fine and the necessity of depositing a copy of the rule in the city archives. To the two sides of the entrance are some small vaulted spaces which served as ossuaries. In this room fragments of stucco reliefs, imitating marble and bearing the portraits of the deceased, were found.

The adjoining building contains sarcophagi and, to the rear, a room with funerary beds on each of its three sides, contained within an arcosolium or niche. On the façade of the monumental building, against which lie a few sarcophagi, are narrow windows created through the use of small rhomboidal-sectioned columns.

Further along the road numerous sarcophagi and a few bases may be seen along the eastern slope. The road curves near tomb 142, which consists of a large exedra, with a square plan, once

Fig. 29 Tomb no. 65 of
Flavia Theophiliane.

Fig. 30
Tomb no. 19 during conservation.

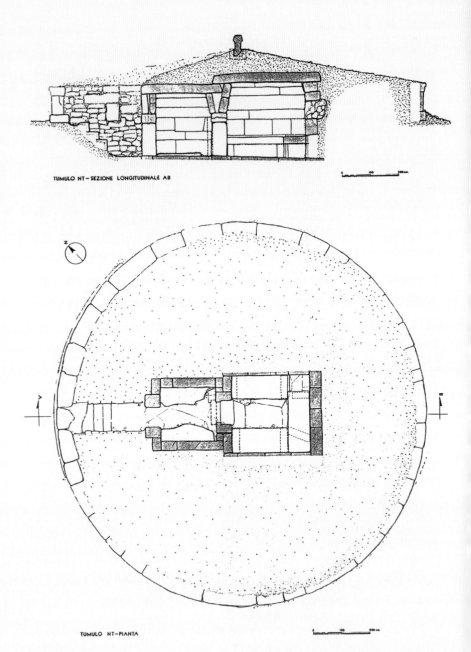

TUMULO NT – SEZIONE LONGITUDINALE AB

TUMULO NT – PIANTA

Fig. 31 Northern necropolis: section and plan of the tumulus tomb NT.

Fig. 32 Northern necropolis: tumulus no. 51.

covered by a barrel-vault, and with an arch decorated with mouldings and capped by a cornice. Up on the right may be seen the
space for a marble tablet that bore the inscription. Even this
example, aside from protecting visitors, probably had the function
of supporting sarcophagi and acting as a *heroon*.

After tomb 142, to the left, are two *bomoì* supporting sarcophagi above a terracing wall. The wild vegetation or *maquis* invades
the ancient enclosures, sprouting between numerous stone coffins
without lids and presenting quite a dramatic image. We may recall
the valley of Jehoshaphat at Jerusalem, which the prophet Joel, in
the Bible, indicates as the site of Universal Judgement.

Along the road the sarcophagi display inscriptions with large
letters, which once were even more evident, having been painted
in red. It is impossible to describe the many aspects of this cemetery

at Hierapolis. The visitor himself will have to search for the various forms of sarcophagus, identifying the more sober decorations of the stone blocks, the floral garlands on the lids, the Gorgon masks and palmettes on the acroteria. He will note the various colours of travertine that change continuously from brown to golden to red, according to the light of day.

Tomb 114 is on the left hand side of the road (fig. 26). Within an enclosure its large *bomòs*, set upon three steps, dominates the coffins to the sides. It is surmounted by a sarcophagus which, though still in place, is broken in two by a violent earthquake. A frame contains the names of Aelius Apollinarios and Neratia Apollonis.

The inscription, composed of 13 lines incised on the face of the tomb, is of quite extraordinary interest: the owner, Aelius Apollinarios Makedon, claims to have built the enclosure and tomb and to have set within it the sarcophagus made of marble from *Thiounta* (modern Gözler), an ancient city nearby, rich in quarries.

The inscription also mentions the fine to be paid to the Gerusia (5.000 denari) by whoever builds close by in such a fashion as to create shadow or obscure the *bomòs* and the sarcophagus. The penalty is even more terrible if one should cancel the inscriptions: "...and he should not enjoy the comfort of offspring or of life! Neither land nor sea should welcome him! He should die without children and suffer every misadventure! And after death the infernal gods should be the angry tormentors of whoever orders construction or tampering and whoever carries out the orders!".

Such a menacing warning has led to this tomb being nick-named the "Tomb of the Curse"!

Fig. 33 Tumuli in the northern necropolis.

One now continues along the road, after having "touched wood", passing a number of sarcophagi aligned on the left. A marble lid in the form of a roof with a lion's head as antefix, funerary erotes as acroteria and the mask of a Gorgon in the tympanum, is worthy of note.

To the right hand side, beneath the level of the present road, is the recently restored tomb 81, which presents the usual scheme of funerary chapel-bomòs, containing rows of funerary beds, a narrow door and an inscription incised in the travertine to the right of the façade. If one can read ancient Greek, one learns that the plot belongs to Eutyches Pompeios, who has left 100 denari towards the performance of the rite of crowning the tomb.

To the left, proceeding up the hill, tomb 65 has a rather low *bomòs* (fig. 29), characterised by a large jutting cornice with a straight profile. On the left hand side are two small openings for the funerary niches. An inscription, eight lines long, is to be found on the side facing the street. It cites the owner Flavia Mettia Theophiliana and recalls the sarcophagus on the roof, in precious Dokimion marble, coming from the Phrygian quarries near Afyon. The usual fine to be paid to the Gerusia and the deposition of the text in the archives are also mentioned.

Arriving at an open space we may note a *bomòs* sustaining two sarcophagi (tomb 56 - fig. 27). Marble slabs with inscriptions are sited to the sides of the door. This is the area in which the greatest concentration of tumuli is to be found. They are also to be seen rising up the slope in a panoramic position. This is the oldest part of the necropolis, dating to Hellenistic times, between the second and first century BC. This type of burial belongs to a much earlier tradition that includes the tumuli of Lydia and Phrygia (the ones of Midas at Gordion are famous, having yielded many objects in precious metal). The families of Hierapolis continued to use tumuli into early Imperial times. Indeed, an inscription of the second century AD records Lucius Salvius Paolinus as owner.

Climbing the barren slope in the same direction, to the side of a cylindrical travertine altar, another tumulus is to seen, noteworthy for the care in which the blocks have been joined. They are particularly well finished in the funerary chamber, in the *dromos* and around the entrance. Further up, two other tumuli dominate the area. Inserted along the perimeter of the largest one (indicated by no. 15; 9.90m in diameter) is a block bearing an inscription. The podium appears to have been dressed with a chisel and presents two niches to the sides of the entrance to contain the lamps that formed part of the funeral cults. Indeed, large numbers of lamps have been discovered nearby and inside all of these buildings.

Fig. 34 Marble statue of sleeping Eros, tied to funerary symbolism. Second century AD.

From this position it is possible to enjoy a splendid panorama of the Lykos valley. Down to the left a small forest of pines and cypresses frames the first major building of the city, the Baths-Basilica, recognisable by its majestic arches. Before the Baths-Basilica, tomb no. 1 may be visited, with its monumental arch opening on the other side of the road. Behind is the funerary chamber that was entered from the right hand side, with door jambs and an architrave surmounted by a relieving arch. The large vaulted roof covered an exedra and offered refuge to relatives who visited the tomb in the occasion of funerary ceremonies and banquets in honour of the dead. Above was a funerary temple *in antis* (only the marble threshold survives) facing the street, which was connected to it by a marble staircase.

Nearby was another *bomòs* (1A), with an inscription dating to the end of the second or beginning of the third century AD, that cites the owner, Marcus Aurelius Stratonicus, and records the fact that a garden was annexed to the burial. Along the joins of the blocks are some large holes cut in medieval times so as to remove and reuse the metal cramps.

In front of the Baths-Basilica, to the right of the road, lies an interesting monument (tomb A6) with a U-shaped podium in which the careful craftsmanship is visible even in the finesse of the cornices. A travertine sarcophagus with an inscription lies to the left, whilst inside the exedra is a partially worked marble coffin decorated with garlands. Tomb A6 lies above a much larger hypogeum or underground chamber, reached from behind the building, which contained the loculi for the burials.

Baths-Basilica [2]

The building has never been fully excavated, though a small excavation around the first archway to the north revealed the *praefurnium* of a hypocaust belonging to a bath building. This earlier construction, in squared travertine blocks, datable to mid Imperial times (second century AD), is also recognisable in the large arches lining the side walls of the building. It may be compared to the vaulted structures of the large Baths in the centre of the city (see 25). The transformation of the bath building *(calidarium)* into a church seems to have taken place in the first half of the sixth century, when Hierapolis was promoted to metropolis of Phrygia Pacatiana.

To the north of the entrance, the new ecclesiastical building also enveloped a rather imposing wall belonging to one of the bath's rooms, so as to create a four-sided portico with square columns. The entrance to the church is formed of two large arches that flank a smaller door surmounted by a relieving arch, rather like the Byzantine city gate (10). In the well preserved main room, six side niches beneath arches are to be seen. In Christian times, dividing walls, crossed by a vaulted passage and crowned by a cornice with a rather schematic profile, were built against the original piers that sustained the arches. The keystones of the arches bear Christian symbols, such as the *chrismon* in a circle, similar to those at the *Martyrion* of St. Philip. The piers divide the nave into three bays, each once covered by a dome or, more likely, by cross-vaults. The apse, constructed in a rougher fashion, with reused irregular masonry, is semicircular on the inside and has a polygonal outer face. This last architectural feature, also present in the apse of the cathedral, is characteristic of micro-Asiatic

Fig. 35 View of the Baths-basilica.

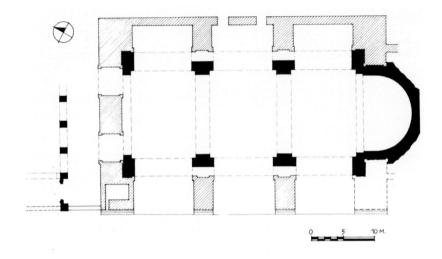

Fig. 36 Plan of the bath building with, in black, the structures pertaining to its transformation into a church.

Fig. 37 Baths-basilica: the large arches of the Roman building, from the west.

Fig. 38 Structure of the Baths-basilica.

architecture, and is also to be found in Italy in the regions that formed part of the Byzantine Empire, such as Ravenna, Sicily and in the territory of Otranto. The church was presumably decorated with fresco painting bearing sumptuous garland motifs, traces of which are to be seen in the intrados of the first arch to the right upon entering the building. The building was destroyed by earthquakes during medieval times as may be seen by cracks in the apse and along the eastern perimeter wall, which is now dangerously unstable and characterised by a strong outwards leaning.

Leaving the Basilica Church, we proceed towards the nearby Frontinus Gate, following the asphalt road. To the right may be seen the

Tomb of Flavius Zeuxis
and Other Funerary Buildings [3]

To the right of the road is a well preserved funerary chapel (Tomb A18), rising above a stepped platform surrounded by a bench (fig.s 41-42). Of rectangular plan, with a two-winged façade, gabled roof and tympanum with a shield, it has a large tapering door with an elegant frame opening in front. The chapel was placed above an underground funerary chamber. The careful workmanship of the travertine blocks suggests a rather early date, perhaps Flavian, when the whole area underwent a programme of monumental building.

A large square construction, covered by a barrel vault, lies behind. It has a threshold block in pink breccia and a cornice moulding on the upper part of the wall which was worked in a rougher fashion than the funerary chapel (A18).

Once again, towards the edge of the plateau, we can see the spectacle provided by the calcareous channels that carry water downhill and form a white cascade of stone in which other funerary buildings are immersed, such as a gabled funerary chapel that appears to be sinking into the calcareous concretions.

On crossing the road to the left hand side, in front of the western tower of the Frontinus Gate, we can see the tomb of Flavius Zeuxis, which was also built during the dynasty of the Flavian Emperors (late first century AD). Even if better built, it recalls the façades along the contemporary Frontinus Street (5) for both building technique and use of the Doric order. The funerary chapel, which contained stone beds, is of rectangular plan and

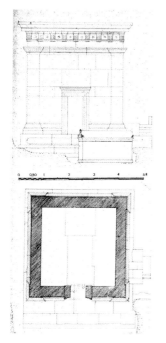

Fig. 40 Tomb of Flavius Zeuxis. End of the first century AD.

Fig. 39 Tomb of Flavius Zeuxis: plan and elevation.

opens onto an enclosure which contained other sarcophagi. The marble sarcophagi, now in the Museum, include one with an inscription recording the girl Maximilla, perhaps daughter of Flavius Zeuxis, and another decorated with erotes that hold garlands and Gorgon masks. At the base of the building is a cornice moulding, whilst the door is preceded by a step with seats. Above the cornice at the entrance is a marble block with an ansate panel upon which is engraved the inscription of the owner, Titus Flavius Zeuxis. He is defined *ergastès* or merchant and the inscription records thirty years of travel in which he took products of Hierapolis (probably the woollen garments for which this area, together with Laodicea, was famous) to Italy, passing Cape Malea, the southernmost tip of the Peleponnese, some 72 times.

The building is crowned with an elegant Doric trabeation, bearing a frieze of metopes and triglyphs containing rosettes.

Behind the Tomb of Flavius Zeuxis appears the round tower of the **Frontinus Gate (4).**

Fig. 41
Tomb no. A 18.

Fig. 42   Tomb no. A 18 and annexed building with a barrel-vault.

Frontinus Gate [4]

This is the monumental entrance to the Roman city and leads onto the large plateia, 14m wide, which crosses the whole settlement, exiting a gate at the opposite side, to connect with the road that goes to *Laodicea* on the Lykos and then *Colossae*.

It is worth admiring the well preserved structure with three openings, in carefully squared travertine blocks, with elegant arches decorated with a simple cornice moulding, flanked by two

Fig. 43 Frontinus Gate.

Fig. 44   Frontinus Gate: western circular tower.

round towers that recall Hellenistic city gates such as that of the Pamphilian city of Perge, near Antalya. The gate opens onto a square in the centre of which are the capping blocks of the large channel that, beneath the *plateia,* collected the rain water and water from the calcareous springs and conducted it out of the city towards the valley. The square is defined to the east by the substructure of the western stoa of the Agora, built of large blocks, and to the west by the enclosure of the funerary monument of Flavius Zeuxis. Various marble fragments from the attic that crowned the sober entrance with three openings, including columns, Corinthian capitals, architraves, are gathered to the northern and western sides of the square of Frontinus.

Fig. 45 Frontinus Gate with the marble dedicatory inscription.

On the two sides of the gate's façade is a monumental marble inscription originally attributed to Caracalla though, following the research and partial restoration by the Italian Archaeological Mission, may now be dated to AD 84 or 86 on the basis of a dedication to the emperor Domitian in the year of his fourth *tribunicia potestas* (tribune magistrate) and twelfth consulate. The dedication is by the proconsul (Roman governor) of Asia Minor, Sextus Julius Frontinus, famous Latin writer and author of the treatise on aqueducts. According to fragments of the inscription, recently discovered reused in late walls built over the *plateia*, it would appear that Frontinus not only built the gate and towers, but also the street. The interest of this figure, the theoretician of Roman hydraulic architecture, for the city of Hierapolis, is not surprising, given its wealth of thermal waters. He was probably also responsible for the construction of the system of channels that drained the waters which, after the collapse and abandonment of the city, invaded the ruins, depositing above them a thick layer of calcareous concretions.

On the southern extremity of the city, a gate with an analogous arrangement of three openings (30), almost certainly built at the same time, constituted a symmetrical monumental entrance, with a similar road flanked by Doric façades.

Having entered the gate it is possible to note the entrances on the inside to the towers, with straightforward jambs and architraves, similar to those of the houses and tombs.

To the left of the entrance are the remains of a small early medieval Byzantine period church, built of reused masonry, with an apsed area in which the marble base of an altar and a marble chancel screen with pierced scale decoration were found. It may have been dedicated to the Virgin Odigitria who protected travellers, and it expresses the sacred nature of entrances that were put under the protection of the divine. Indeed, on the right pier of the central arch of the façade of the Frontinus Gate is a rectangular indentation that must have held a marble tablet with an image of a deity, perhaps Apollo, the protector of the city. Even if in medieval times the entrance to the city was the Byzantine Gate, the three openings and towers of the Frontinus Gate still formed a significant settlement limit to whoever approached the site from the north.

Fig. 46   Aerial view of the Frontinus gate and street. In the centre is the tomb of Flavius Zeuxis.

Frontinus Street [5]

The principal street *(plateia)*, 14 metres wide, appears through its architectural characteristics to have been conceived as a part of a unitary project together with the gate. It is paved and has pavements. In the centre runs the main drain covered with large stone blocks. Along the sides are a number of buildings comprising houses, shops and warehouses, unified by a travertine façade which is 170 metres long and terminates at the so-called Byzantine Gate built at the beginning of the fifth century. The

Fig. 47 View of the Street of Frontinus at the beginning of the excavations.

Fig. 48
View of the Street of Frontinus after the excavations (1994).

façade of the buildings fronting the street is of Doric order with piers and adjoining half columns, capitals with echinus and abacus, and trabeation and frieze with metopes and triglyphs.

The excavation of the *plateia*, up to the Byzantine Gate, has been one of the most difficult undertakings of the Mission as the road surface was covered not only by the rubble collapse of the buildings, but also by a thick calcareous deposit which, at times, was up to two metres thick. It had formed through the runoff of spring water that, no longer constrained by the Roman drainage system, forged its natural path through the rubble covering the large *plateia*. The lengthy use of pneumatic compressors, which slowly broke the calcareous formations into fragments, was the only way in which the street could be brought to light.

Fig. 49 Along the Street of Frontinus.

Fig. 50   Marble pilaster with a representation of Hercules, found along the Street of Frontinus.

77

Fig. 51 Doric façade in travertine along the Street of Frontinus, west side.

Fig. 52 Blaundus: Doric façade in travertine.

Fig. 53 Graphic reconstruction of the Frontinus Street (R. Rachini).

To the sides of the street may be seen the entrances, with travertine door jambs and architraves, to the various buildings, warehouses and shops. The Doric trabeation of the façade presents a continuous alignment of square holes which served to insert the wooden poles of a portico that rested on a colonnade along the pavement. This was a late addition, of the fourth century AD, making use of various reused materials, so as to create shade along the street. On the right hand side a series of buildings, clearly of late date (ninth-tenth century) for the architectural technique making use of old stone blocks and tiles, invades the road surface. Despite the rather unattractive rough building technique employed, these rooms form an important historical document illustrating the radical transformation of this area following the construction of the city walls after the public buildings of the first century AD were transformed into private houses, without any respect for the street, now reduced to no more than eight metres in width.

Latrine [6]

To the left hand side of the street, immediately after the Byzantine church, a particularly well-preserved building may be noted, inserted into the unitary Doric façade lining the street. It was discovered in a state of collapse, clearly caused by an earthquake, that has allowed its almost complete reconstruction. The restoration, still in progress, has permitted the anastilosis of the rear wall with squared blocks. Even the piers of the façade have been reconstructed and put back into their original position, together with the monolithic screens between one pier and the other, and the architrave and cornice.

The building, 6.30 metres wide and 20.50 metres long, was reached by a side entrance through a square vestibule that opened onto the street. From the two side doors, down three steps, the

Fig. 54 Façade of the Flavian latrine after restoration, 1997.

Fig. 55
Rubble of the latrine that collapsed due to an earthquake, seen from a balloon.

Fig. 56 The collapse of the latrine on the road.

Fig. 57   The latrine: identification of the bases of the façade pilasters after excavation.

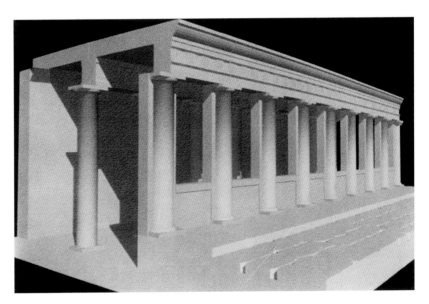

Fig. 58   Reconstruction of the latrine in AUTOCAD.

Fig. 59 Conservation of the Doric façades along the Frontinus Street.

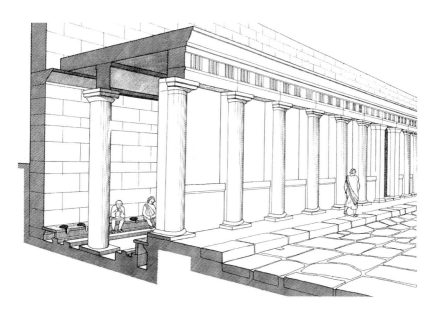

Fig. 60 Graphic reconstruction of the latrine (R. Rachini).

Fig. 61   Red painted inscription on a pier along the Frontinus Street,
with an acclamation to the Emperor Justinian.

original level may be reached. It lies at least one metre below
street level. The single long room is divided longitudinally into two
aisles by a row of monolithic Doric columns that supported a roof
composed of large, heavy, travertine blocks. The excavation has
permitted us to identify the building as a public latrine, with a
drain that ran along the two long sides, sluicing the liquids into
the main drain or *cloaca* beneath the Frontinus Street. Along the
perimeter walls may be seen the groove into which the seats with
holes were fitted, whilst in front of the principal drain is a small
channel in which clean running water was available for hygiene.

The paving is composed of travertine slabs which display
heavy signs of wear and corrosion. The building is an example of
a public latrine, remarkable for its size and chronology (end of the

first century AD) and for its position in correspondence with the entrance to the city and to the immense Agora, rather like the comparable example at Side that dates slightly later (second century AD). The monumental façade facing the street does not conflict with the public function of this building (at Side the latrine was decorated with statues). Just like the baths and nymphaea, the latrines were a sign of prestige for the city indicating the social services offered to its inhabitants.

A particularly precious piece of evidence for the dating of the collapse of this building and of the earthquake that provoked it comes from the red painted inscriptions found on the half-columns of its façade, bearing acclamations to the emperor Justinian. They may have been painted on the occasion of a visit by him to the city, as a welcome placed just after the entrance through the honorary gate. At this late date the concept of public hygiene was far more approximate, and the building was no longer used as a latrine, but had been converted into a storeroom for hay and stables for mules. Indeed, on the back wall are a number of holes cut so as to be able to tie the pack animals. The excavation of the building revealed abundant traces of a fire that had led to its abandonment prior to its final collapse.

Continuing towards the end of the Frontinus Street, and turning to the right before the Byzantine Gate, amongst the late walls that occupy the Flavian shops, it is possible to make out the "Tomba Bella" *(7).*

"Tomba Bella" [7]

The monument was built within an enclosure composed of rectangular slabs, which had been particularly well cut and joined. In the centre is the stepped podium, also in carefully smoothed travertine blocks, whilst close by are various fragments of the cornice that formed part of the marble revetment of the podium. The marble sarcophagus decorated with garlands, now in the

Fig. 62 Restoration of the "Tomba Bella".

86

Museum (see p. 212), lay within a marble aedicula above the podium. It is one of the masterpieces of Anatolian sculpture of the first half of the first century AD. The whole building formed a heroon or funerary monument that, by elevating the deceased to heroic status, must have honoured a particularly famous member of the city's population whose identity, unfortunately, is not known, as no inscription has yet come to light. This building was set within a cemetery, as is indicated by the discovery of simple tombs cut into the bedrock, and was respected even after the earthquake of AD 60 when the entire area was transformed so as to build the shops and the Frontinus Street, evidently because of the significance of the tomb's occupant as regards the city.

Fig. 63 The "Tomba Bella" after restoration.

Fig. 64 The relief of the "Tomba Bella"; Julio-Claudian or first half of the first century AD

Fig. 65 Detail of the "Tomba Bella" with the incoronation of the deceased as a hero.

Returning to the Frontinus Street to the left, passing by the alignment of shops, we reach a large open area, which is bordered to the left by a cypress grove that occupies the northern half of the ancient Agora. Here we may take rest from the sun, observing the flight of the hoopoe, broken by the lament of the turtledoves that nest in the uppermost branches of the trees.

Agora [8]

The Frontinus Street with its shops, warehouses and other functional buildings, was only part of a far more ambitious reorganisation of this area, as part of a reconstruction project following the Neronian earthquake of AD 60. The vast area between the *plateia* and the mountain slopes to the east, which hosted a number

Fig. 66 Agora, western colonnade.

of cave tombs, was transformed into an immense square which is probably to be identified with the commercial Agora of Hierapolis. There are no certain indications of the existence of the civic Agora, which must have been in the centre of the city, probably close to the large baths and the Temple of Apollo. It is likely that it was totally buried by the calcareous deposits that invaded the whole area that now lies in front of the Pamukkale Motel.

Before the Neronian earthquake, the area of the commercial Agora lay outside the settlement and was occupied by the necropolis and various industrial establishments. Trial excavations carried out along the eastern side of the square have bought to light some circular kilns for the production of pottery, with dumps of ceramic wasters of Megarian ware, a relief decorated pottery dating between the second and first century BC. Amongst the finds were a number of mould fragments used to produce the relief decoration that consisted of floral motifs, as well as masks, and mythological and Dionysian figures, proving the local production of these vases. During the course of the second century AD, one of the largest squares of Asia Minor and of the whole antique world was created in this area, measuring about 170 metres in width and 280 metres in length, higher than the Frontinus Street and abutting the eastern side of the rocky slopes. Here lay the most majestic buildings that had already been seen and described by travellers in the last century. P. Laborde, in particular, had drawn the characteristic Ionic capitals with bearded masks. Towards the end of the 1950's, P. Verzone conducted some trial excavations, through which he recognised the structures of the *Sebasteion*, the building dedicated to the Imperial cult. Systematic research begun in 1979, allowing the definition of the extent of the entire monumental area, as well permitting a certain amount of restoration and organisation of the marble blocks brought to light.

For those coming from the Frontinus Street, it is possible to observe the vast overburden created by centuries of colluvial deposition that has covered the ruins and the original level of the square beneath some three metres of gravel and clay. In the northern half of the square is a small wood of cypress trees that impedes vision of the remains of all the buildings that surrounded the Agora. The plan is to excavate the area and to reconstruct the tree cover at the original level of the Roman square, thus allowing the possibility to see the structures on all four sides, together with a pleasant layout of the trees that offer shade and make the visit less tiresome.

West side

Excavations along the western side have brought to light the remains of a large marble portico, 14 metres wide, with an Ionic façade and an internal row of Corinthian columns, of which some capitals characterised by a careful plastic rendering of the acanthus leaves and of the elegant spiral helixes remain. In the northern part, a reconstruction of some 15 metres in length allows a better idea of this monumental structure that also surrounded the square on its northern and southern sides. An earthen fill has been used to reconstruct the original ground level of the stoa, which had been severely cut by holes and robber trenches excavated during the fifth and sixth centuries so as to obtain building material. The stylobate with its steps has been reconstructed in correspondence with the façade, using some of the original marble blocks. Some of the Ionic bases, together with a short length of

Fig. 67 Agora, west side: the discovery of a Corinthian capital.

91

the elegant trabeation consisting of the architrave block in three bands, with a frieze of floral scrolls surmounted by a row of ovolos and a highly pronounced cornice with dentils, have been placed upon the stylobate. On the inside of the stoa, the higher Corinthian columns had a double spacing with respect to the Ionic façade. Each column was sited on its own foundations, composed of large superimposed travertine blocks that were set directly upon the natural rock base, reaching a depth of up to three metres. Various column fragments and Corinthian capitals discovered in the area, generally found re-employed in Byzantine walls, have been set upon the bases of the original alignment of the Corinthian colonnade.

The stoa must have suffered great damage during an earthquake, probably in the second half of the fourth century AD, and in succeeding centuries the area was occupied by workshops for the production of tiles and bricks, with their circular kilns set within rectangular walled structures. The houses of the craftsmen grew-up alongside the workshops. So as to reconcile these new buildings with the lower level of the Frontinus Street onto which the entrances opened, the level of the stoa was lowered by excavating the earthen fill of the porticoes and removing the blocks. In this way, only part of the foundations and sporadic pieces of marble reused in late antique buildings survive to document the gigantic colonnades that stretched for hundreds of metres.

Towards the centre of the western side may be seen the structures of Byzantine houses (tenth-eleventh centuries) with rooms arranged around courtyards. These document the ruralisation of the city during the last phases of its existence. To even more recent times, perhaps Ottoman, belong the structures of a domestic complex, grouped within an enclosure, that lie to the north and

Fig. 68 Agora, west side: the discovery of marble columns.

Fig. 69 Agora, west side: remains of coloured marbles inlays.

Fig. 70 Agora, west side: the discovery of Byzantine ceramics of the fifth-sixth century.

Fig. 71   Agora, west side: the discovery of the statue of Attis in 1997.

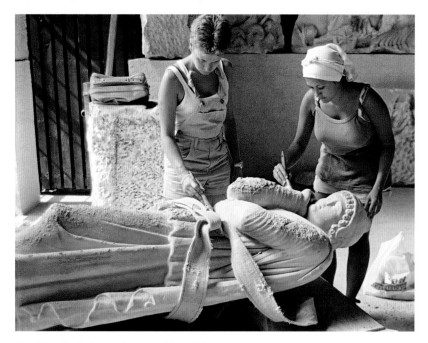

Fig. 72   Preliminary cleaning of the statue.

Fig. 73
The statue of Attis; end of
the second century AD

partly overly the Byzantine buildings. These may be compared to
recent rural Turkish houses that may be seen in the villages of the
surrounding territory.

Proceeding along the western stoa up to the north angle, a
brief stretch of the stylobate is preserved, with a marble step upon
which is set part of a column shaft with an Ionic capital (unfortunately broken) belonging to the façade. At this point it is possible

Fig. 74   Agora: graphic reconstruction of the western stoa (R. Rachini).

to see how the classical structures where even more radically demolished in medieval times so as to create a route towards the valley for the running water which from the Byzantine Gate had been channelled towards the Agora for agricultural purposes.

North side

The Ionic marble stoa continued along the northern side of the Agora. Here, the façade has been freed of earth, and the colonnade may be seen to have been largely destroyed, presenting large gaps right down to the foundations. It is better preserved only at its eastern end, where the bases of the monolithic columns are still in place, being reused in later structures. The marble cornices belonging to the façade of the portico have been aligned in front of the stylobate. The sima is decorated with lion's heads, not particularly well sculpted, which recall ancient dripstones.

Various late structures (fifth-sixth centuries) built of bricks and reused marble and travertine are preserved in the central part of the stoa. They belong to a pottery production area with workshops, houses for the artisans and various round kilns, contemporary with those of the west stoa. Many lime mixing pits have also been found, associated with kilns for transforming marble into lime.

Impressive traces of the earthquake that provoked the definitive abandonment of the city in the first half of the seventh century may be seen in both these structures and the travertine channels. The stylobate of the stoa is broken, is out of alignment at various points and displays quite startling differences in level through subsidence. The fifth-sixth century walls and pavements also display large cracks, as do the rather resistant travertine channels, all testimony to the violence of the tremors.

Fig. 75 Agora: north side.

East side

On the east side are the preserved remains of the monumental stoa-basilica which dominated the square of the Agora for a length of 280 metres. The remains of the marble staircase (4 meters high) that led down from the stoa-basilica to the surface of the square, can be admired, especially in the southern part. Just like the other parts of the building, this was demolished in the course of the fifth and sixth centuries, and the operation of demolition is well documented through the excavation. The construction technique of the staircase is visible in the transverse walls of rough but solid masonry that contained an earth fill and supported the marble blocks of the stairs. A short length of the staircase has been reconstructed in the original fashion, though using travertine blocks where the marble is missing, thus giving an idea of what the original structure must have looked like.

The building had a two storey façade, a portico with square-sectioned piers with adjoining semi-columns, fluted on their upper half, with Ionic type bases and Ionic capitals bearing bearded masks at their angles in correspondence with the pilasters (see Museum p. 211). A dado with architrave and a frieze with garlands that frame Dionysian type masks and a large cornice decorated with dentils and rows of palmettes, upon which rested the succession of arches, may be seen. The upper floor had a row of piers with half columns in a reddish breccia stone, with more schematic Corinthian capitals in white marble. The effects of chromatic contrast and chiaroscuro, together with the rich decoration, were accentuated in the central part of the stoa-basilica which formed the monumental entrance. The detailed analysis of the foundations and the systematic study of the marble fragments have allowed us to graphically reconstruct this part of the building, composed of two advanced sections to the sides of the

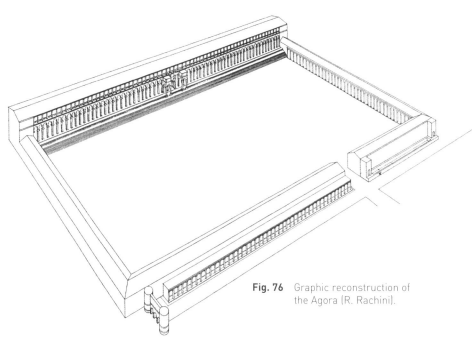

Fig. 76 Graphic reconstruction of the Agora (R. Rachini).

Fig. 77 Agora: stoa-basilica and staircase on the eastern side.

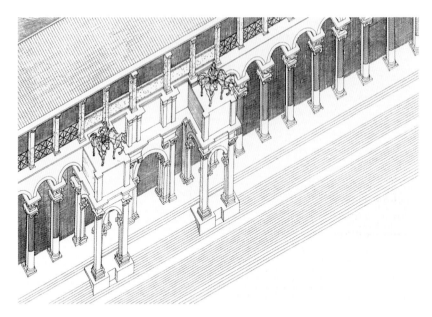

Fig. 78 Graphic reconstruction of the central body of the eastern stoa (M.P. Rossignani, R. Rachini).

entrance surmounted by an arch. The entranceway seems to have been characterised by an extraordinary Baroque decoration in the piers that held large Corinthian columns with acanthus leaves framing erotes with garlands. The piers were tied to arches which, in turn, were supported by complex figurative features composed of capitals with lions savaging bulls, upon which were set sphinxes (see Museum, p. 211). The whole was characterised by a great strength of expression.

The stoa-basilica was twenty metres wide, though we do not know if it was divided into long naves by one or more rows of columns. The rear wall, behind which extended the eastern necropolis, had adjoining half-columns in travertine with marble Ionic capitals similar to those in the façade. A sarcophagus with inscription abuts it on the outside.

Fig. 79
Agora, east side: anastilosis
of a pilaster of the façade.

Fig. 80
Agora, east side: discovery
of an Ionic capital
decorated with masks.

Fig. 81
Agora, east side:
view from a balloon.

Fig. 82
Element from the
stoa-basilica with
garland decoration.

Fig. 83 Façade of the stoa-basilica: figural capital of lions savaging bulls.

Fig. 84
Element from the
stoa-basilica with the
figure of a Sphinx.

103

Fig. 85
Figure of a Sphinx from
the stoa-basilica.

Fig. 86
Stoa-basilica:
architectural
cornice with
the figure of a
gladiator.

Fig. 87 Decorative mask from the Ionic capitals.

Fig. 88
Meerschaum pipe with
decorative mask from
capitals of the Agora
(Mahmut Özsak,
Eskişehir).

This building is better preserved in its central part. It is clear that after its abandonment following the fourth century earthquake, demolition began at the two extremities and, fortunately for us, lost intensity towards the centre. The excavation has brought to light the foundations of the frontal piers, consisting of large superimposed blocks reaching down to the bedrock, as well as those of the piers that stood proud of the façade, belonging to the central entranceway of the immense building.

At the moment, a programme of re-systemisation of the blocks is underway, with the reconstitution of the pier drums and other architectural features, and the anastilosis of one of the piers discovered in collapse. One of its drums has been substituted by a modern copy, given the bad state of conservation of the original. The imposing nature of the reconstructed pier gives an idea of the grandiose marble façade of the stoa-basilica which, with its two storeys, reached a height of some twenty metres.

South side

The southern side of the Agora is less visible than the others as it is buried even deeper by the colluvial deposits. A fairly large excavation in the centre of this side has permitted the discovery of the ancient level of the square at about four metres below present ground level. The fifth century Byzantine fortifications run along this side of the Agora. As may be seen from the excavations, they were founded upon the stylobate of the façade of the portico that ran for 170 metres in length, closing this side of the square. At the base of the Byzantine wall, which was constructed with blocks of travertine and other materials derived from the demolition of the Agora, may be seen the marble step upon which the colonnade had originally been based as well as a row of collapsed marble cornice blocks with leonine protomes, similar to those found on the northern side of the square. It is clear that the Agora was destroyed by a strong earthquake prior to the construction of the Byzantine city walls, quite probably during the second half of the fourth century AD. The crisis that followed impeded the reconstruction of the large Agora complex, which was far too expensive, and it was thus left out of the new fifth century wall circuit, to be used as a quarry for the travertine blocks used in the wall's construction, whilst the marble fragments were largely turned into lime in the numerous lime-kilns found in the area. Indeed, along the eastern side of the square, close to the entrance of the stoa-basilica, there are large accumulations of smashed marble, resulting from the fragmentation of the blocks so that they could be easily transported to the kilns. Names were summarily incised on the collapsed pier blocks, perhaps representing magistrates, as a sign of possession of the various

Fig. 89   Agora, south side: Byzantine walls built above the marble stylobate of the stoa).

Fig. 90 Decorated architrave with the head of a Gorgon from the southern side of the Agora.

materials to be reused. The name *Florentios*, preceded by a cross, may be read on the restored pier. The Byzantine wall also suffered serious damage by the seventh century earthquake, to judge both by the collapsed masonry along its course and by signs of instability along the bottom of the standing remains.

What was the role of the great Agora complex? It is easy to imagine it as a commercial centre, given its position at the entrance to the city and its close link with the shops and ware-houses along the Frontinus Street. However, as other gigantic multi-functional structures built in Imperial times, it must also have served other functions. The large stoa-basilica, judging from the dedications to the emperors, may have had spaces reserved for the Imperial cult. Another function seems to be ever more supported by the evidence: the use of the area for athletic games and gladiatorial combat. Inscriptions that document the ecumenical games in honour of Apollo Pythios have come to light in this area, whilst certain architectural features from the central part of the stoa-basilica bear the illustration of a gladiator with the incised name *Chrysopteros* (golden wings) (fig. 86). The staircase may have been used as seating for the spectators, and the fact that the floor of the square was not paved with stone or marble, but composed of beaten earth, leads one to believe that the area was used for both sporting competitions and gladiatorial combat. The length of the area, some 280 metres, is comparable with that of the stadium at Aphrodisias. An inscription from Hierapolis refers to a stadium which has never been discovered, even through use of aerial photographs. Should we perhaps identify the Agora also as the city stadium?

Chronological table for the Agora:

Second-first century BC:
> necropolis; artisinal area for the production of coarse pottery and "Megarian ware" vases with relief decoration.

First century AD:
> portico abutting the eastern hill, with a religious function?

AD 60: destruction by earthquake.

Flavian period (end of the first century AD):
> beginning of reorganisation of the area.

Second century AD (from Hadrian to Antoninus Pius):
> realisation of the large complex with *stoai* and the stoa-basilica.

Second half of the fourth century:
> destruction by earthquake.

Fifth and sixth century:
> construction of the Byzantine wall along the southern limit of the Agora, with blocks taken from the *stoai*; lime and pottery kilns along the northern and western sides.

First half of the seventh century:
> earthquake that causes the collapse of the Byzantine wall and other buildings, and abandonment of the whole area.

Tenth to twelfth century:
> rural houses along the western side.

Ottoman times:
> rural houses amongst the ruins along the north-western side.

To the north-east of the Agora, towards the hills, we may see some stepped remains clinging to the rocky slope:

The Suburban Theatre [9]

These are the badly preserved remains of a theatre which it has not yet been possible to explore. A preliminary analysis has assigned the monument to Hellenistic times. It appears to have been sited at a considerable distance from the city-centre that gravitated around the Temple of Apollo. Preserved features include parts of the travertine seats, the rectilinear walls of the *analemma*, and part of a channel that, passing beneath the cavea, drained natural water from the slopes following a technique similar, though on a smaller scale, to that employed in the stadium at Nyssa on the Meander, which was built on substructures crossing a river valley. No traces of the stage building remain. It is worth noting that the *analemma* wall is built of the same blocks with concave mouldings and terminal fillets as those used for the seats.

Fig. 91 Remains of the suburban theatre.

Continuing up the hill, on the summit, may be seen an interesting funerary monument known as the "Tomb of the Loner", from which there is a splendid view of the city and the Lykos valley. On top of the funerary chamber cut into the rock stood a travertine obelisk which now lies in pieces and which, together with the cavea of the theatre, constituted a sort of meridian of a large solar clock.

One then returns towards the Frontinus Street, in the direction of the entrance to the city, where there are the two square towers of the Byzantine Gate in large travertine blocks, over which scurry large lizards and where the activity of the black and grey woodpecker may be seen, intent on using its long beak to snatch the insects attracted by its loud trill from the holes and interstices in the stone.

The North Byzantine Gate [10]

The north gate forms part of a fortification system built at Hierapolis in Theodosian times (end of the fourth century AD) and is its monumental entrance, matched by a symmetrical gate to the south of the city. Built of reused material from the demolition of the Agora, it is flanked by two square towers, as in other nearby cities such as Blaundus.

The dangerously cracked monolithic blocks of the architrave have recently been consolidated through insertion of a metal structure, after which the entranceway has been cleared of the thick calcareous deposit that blocked it. The gate is characterised by an elegant relieving arch that serves to lighten the load of the wall above the architrave. Like the other Christian period buildings, it is decorated by a circle enclosing a cross-like symbol. Christian symbols *(chrismon)* also appear on the two marble brackets that support the architrave of the façade.

Fig. 92 Aerial view of the Byzantine gate and walls. Fifth century AD

Fig. 93 North Byzantine gate.

Fig. 94 Graphic reconstruction of the Byzantine north gate (R. Rachini).

Four large marble brackets with heads of lions, of a panther and of a Gorgon were found collapsed in front of the gate. They are quite expressive and, whilst belonging to antique buildings, were evidently reused as apotropaic elements on the two sides of the gate so as to ward off evil influence. The phenomenon of reusing ancient sculpture is attested in other Byzantine gates such as that at the citadel of St. John at Ephesus. Of the four brackets, two have been temporarily placed to the right of the entrance, whilst the others are visible in the courtyard of the Museum.

The Byzantine City Walls [11]

These were erected between the end of the fourth and the beginning of the fifth century following the Imperial decrees of Theodosius and Arcadius of AD 395 and 396. They are not particularly imposing, measuring only 2,50m in width. It appears that they were built in haste, with reused blocks from the demolition of many public buildings, in particular from the porticoes of the Agora and the nearby suburban theatre. The circuit encompassed most of the Roman city, following the ups and downs of the terrain, and defended the strategic points with 24 square towers lying at an average distance of eighty metres from each other. The two principal gates, each with a single entrance flanked by two square towers, correspond to the two extremities of the *plateia*. Along the eastern side are two postern gates, surmounted by flat lintels with relieving arches, that lead to the *martyrion*

Fig. 95 Byzantine walls with a postern gate, east side.

of St. Philip and to the eastern necropolis. Along the north in particular, the circuit engulfs parts of ancient buildings that may be distinguished through the more regular appearance of their blocks: they include the Nymphaeum of the Tritons and, further east, another building with squared travertine blocks belonging to the southern portico of the Agora. Recent excavations in this area, after the removal of thick colluvial deposits, have brought to light a tract of the walls standing to a height of 4.10 metres. It is based on the stylobate of the south stoa of the Agora which, when the wall was built, had already fallen down due to an earthquake as may be seen in the marble cornice blocks still in their original state of collapse. The walls also cut the clay pipes that were used to transport water from the *castellum aquae* (reservoir) to the Nymphaeum of the Tritons.

The structure contains reused blocks of various forms and dimensions, including marble, which, however, was not common as it was usually burnt to produce lime. Further uphill, to the east, many travertine seats may be seen to have been employed in the structure, clearly coming from the suburban theatre which, like the Agora, was also systematically dismantled. These were the two main building complexes that remained outside of the wall circuit, and both had been gravely damaged by the earthquake.

In the section of wall excavated, as in the entire circuit, there are traces of substantial collapses provoked by a second, more recent, earthquake, referable to the first half of the seventh century, that destroyed the entire city. It must have been of quite exceptional violence, given the substantial lesions that mark even the most resistant blocks and which, in more than one place, led to subsidence creating remarkable differences in height with respect to the original level of the foundations.

Upon returning to the Byzantine Gate and having crossed the threshold, we may observe that the wall structure abuts the angle of a vast monument that opens onto the plateia to the left:

The Nymphaeum of the Tritons [12]

The realisation of the monumental Nymphaeum of the Tritons, so-called because of the presence of reliefs of these mythical figures in the act of sounding sea trumpets and other musical instruments, was included in the ambitious building programme intended to reorganise the entrance to the city. The presence of a large fountain was indispensable so as to provide water to the caravans at the end of their long journey along the Meander valley, and this necessity was satisfied with the usual architectural magnificence. Hierapolis was not lacking in water, as an epigram incised on the wall of the diazoma of the theatre tells us: "From Asia, rich in its

Fig. 96   Nymphaeum of the Tritons and plateia.

Fig. 97
Nymphaeum of the
Tritons: aerial view. The
collapse of the back wall.

Fig. 98
Nymphaeum of the
Tritons: architectural
decoration in place.

Fig. 99 a-b Nymphaeum of the Tritons: architrave with the dedicatory inscription to Alexander Severus.

rivers, you can enjoy the most excellent earth, Hierapolis, golden city, Lady of the Nymphs, adorned with splendid springs". Nevertheless, the calcareous water from the thermal springs was not drinkable, and a system of aqueducts had to tap water from springs further up the hills.

The Nymphaeum of the Tritons, together with that of the Temple (16), is one of the two big monumental fountains of the city, with a street frontage some 60 metres long. It is composed of a façade with two short wings that house niches for statues. Remains of the marble trabeation of the lower order are preserved in place on the two lateral travertine walls, and are composed of an architrave, frieze and cornice, displaying typical stylistic characteristics of the third century AD. The entire back wall of the nymphaeum, which had later been incorporated into the Byzantine wall, had collapsed backwards because of the earthquakes. Various architectural fragments lie in the area, belying a sumptuous decoration, typical of Imperial period nymphaea particularly in Asia Minor including Aspendos, Perge, Side and Miletus. The pieces include pediments with Tritons, piers and architraves. Systematic excavation of the monument, beginning in 1993 and continuing in succeeding years, have brought to light the fragments of figured and architectural decoration in marble, which had collapsed into the large basin that opened to the street. Numerous marble slabs with scenes of the Amazonomachy have been found, similar to those of the parapet of the nymphaeum of Aphrodisias, as well as other pediments with Tritons, dolphins and Erotes riding fish. Of particular interest is the presence of further marble slabs with figures of bearded men and girls, reclining in a great variety of poses on rocks, holding large overturned vases from which gushes water. They are personifications of rivers and springs, an appropriate theme for this type of building (fig. 104). The reliefs, which

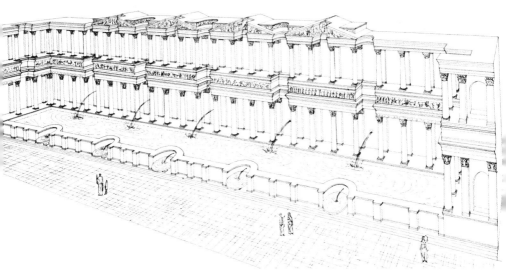

Fig. 100 Hypothetical reconstruction of the Nymphaeum of the Tritons (F. Ghio, L. Campagna).

Fig. 101 Discovery of a marble relief with the Amazonomachy, from the Nymphaeum of the Tritons - 1994.

Fig. 102 Tympanum of the Nymphaeum with a Triton holding a musical instrument.

Fig. 103 Nymphaeum of the Tritons: marble relief showing the battle between Amazons and Greeks.

Fig. 104
Relief with a river-god,
from the Nymphaeum
of the Tritons.

Fig. 105
Relief showing the
fight between an
Amazon and a Greek,
from the Nymphaeum
of the Tritons.

Fig. 106 Relief with an Amazon, from the Nymphaeum of the Tritons.

Fig. 107 Aerial view of the Nymphaeum of the Tritons before the start of excavations.

Fig. 108   Lifting blocks at the Nymphaeum of the Tritons.

were sculpted locally, are stylistically similar to those of the theatre and may be assigned to the same workshop. An important discovery for the dating of the building is that of the architrave blocks that were positioned on the first order of the colonnade. They bear a Greek inscription that dedicates the building to Good Fortune, to Apollo Archegetes and to the emperor Alexander Severus, who reigned from AD 222 to 235, in a period of particular growth for Hierapolis. Indeed, only a few years before, during the reign of Elagabalus, the city had received the title of *neokoros* or "custodian of the temple" of the cult of the Emperor. The complexity and richness of the monumental façades of the nymphaea recall those of entrance gates to *agorai*, such as that of Miletus, as well as the stages of theatres. These buildings were, in a way, associated. Indeed, the nymphaeum was called the "*theatrum aquae*" in antiquity. The sprays of water that splashed against statues, reliefs and capitals, created quite a spectacle, following a concept that we may see repeated in famous Baroque fountains in Rome, such as those of Piazza Navona or the Fontana di Trevi.

After the Nymphaeum of the Tritons, to the left, along the line of the Byzantine walls, is an excavated area corresponding to:

The Byzantine Baths [13]

This is a building complex, not fully excavated, which construction is dateable to the fifth-sixth century AD, immediately after the building of the Byzantine walls. The building was erected above the rubble and demolition debris of the south stoa of the Agora. The bathing complex, separated from the Byzantine walls by a narrow road, appears to have been public, also because of its position close to the entrance to the city, just after the gate and the nymphaeum. An apsed room is visible, with plastered basins and a floor supported by the *suspensurae* of a hypocaust, which leads us to interpret the room as a *calidarium*. It presumably had a vaulted ceiling composed of bricks, including the various fragments discovered in the excavated rubble. The continuance of the excavations should allow us to define the plan of the complex, which constitutes a rare document for the transition between the Imperial Roman public baths, usually of monumental scale, and medieval baths which were common in the Islamic world. The abandonment of the building may be dated, on archaeological grounds, to the earthquake of the first half of the seventh century that destroyed the city.

Fig. 109   Byzantine baths: praefurnium.

Fig. 110   Byzantine baths: calidarium.

Returning to the nymphaeum of the Tritons and crossing the plateia to the west we reach the ruins of a building where one may recognise a

Podium in Travertine [14]

This monument has never been excavated, though the emerging ruins show an ashlar wall in travertine, surmounted by a cornice moulding similar to those of the funerary chapels in the necropolis. Later additions may be identified in the walls built of smaller blocks bonded with mortar. The remains probably belong to a vast thermal complex probably referable to the first century AD.

Fig. 111   Podium in travertine.

Retracing our steps, in correspondance with a break in the high channel which stands proud of the ground surface and which follows the line of the main street, are the remains of one of the principal buildings of the Christian city:

The Cathedral [15]

The building was linked to the *plateia* by a narthex and an atrium of which various features may be seen, in particular those pertaining to the north and south porticoes and the two doors that opened into the narthex. From the narthex, to the right, one enters the baptistery, a rectangular apsed building, perhaps divided

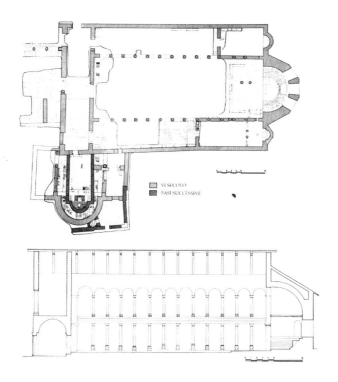

Fig. 112 Plan and section of the Cathedral with its baptistery.

129

Fig. 113   Apse of the Cathedral with seats of the synthronon.

by columns into three naves. The circular baptismal font, with steps down two sides and revetted with marble, was discovered in the apsidal area. The building's function was maintained in medieval times, though it was reduced in dimensions by the construction within the original shell of a hall with a smaller apse, whose pavement covered the baptismal font.

Returning through the narthex, one may enter the church through one of the three doors corresponding to the nave and aisles. The large hall is divided by two rows of columns, surmounted by elegant capitals with water leaves of Pergamene type. The trabeation supported a second order of columns that opened onto the clerestories, with various types of Ionic capitals and impost blocks. The roof was composed of a wooden framework with tiles. The apse, as in the extra-urban church (2), is of circular plan on the inside and polygonal on the outside, with three large arched windows which occupy almost all the widths of the sides of the external polygon. The interior of the main apse is occupied by the *synthronon*, the stepped semicircular benches reserved for the clergy and the bishop during the liturgy. Part of the original pavement is preserved in the right aisle, and is composed of *opus sectile* or polychrome marble tiles forming a geometric pattern, a typical technique commonly found in late antique public and private buildings. The parallels of the clerestory capitals with the Justinianic capitals from the church of St. John at Ephesus indicate a date in the first half of the sixth century. In medieval times two chapels were inserted, through blocking the colonnades and inserting two small apses in the side aisles.

From the cathedral we head towards the centre of the city, marked by the imposing remains of the Baths, crossing the extensive area of rubble from collapsed houses in which we may distinguish door jambs still in place, walls of various buildings and partially excavated stretches of side streets, with travertine slabs that cover channels of the drainage system and pottery pipes that distributed drinking water throughout the city. It is quite a suggestive walk that allows us to observe the natural flora and fauna that populates the landscape of stones and earth, with large lizards of the same colour as the travertine, tortoises, owls that nest amongst the ruins and crested larks with their brown crests that hurry across the open spaces.

Before reaching the Pamukkale Motel, we turn left towards the hill to see the large wall of the:

Temple Nymphaeum [16]

It has a U-shaped plan with two wings that enclosed the large basin. The lower part is built of more regularly-shaped travertine blocks, whilst the upper part has blocks of varying dimensions, clearly reused. The walls are remarkably thick (central walls: 4m; side walls: 3m) and are built of blocks of various shape, such as the Doric semi-columns that belonged to the portico adjoining the peribolos of the Temple of Apollo at the point at which it was demolished to make way for the nymphaeum. Marble artefacts were also reused in the wall, including two statues of priestesses and fragments of the frieze and of the Doric architrave from the first century AD portico that surrounded the Temple peribolos. The back wall of the nymphaeum bears the cavity in which the marble trabeation of the lower order was lodged, and also displays three rectangular niches (the central one with a hole for a water pipe) and the alternately curved and straight base, crowned by a marble cornice formed of blocks marked with Greek letters that helped guide their assembly.

On the basis of the architectural fragments it has been possible to create a hypothetical reconstruction of the two orders, a lower one with exedras along the base, and an upper one with linear tracts that are alternately projecting and recessed.

In correspondence with the curves of the lower order, the niches where surmounted by tympana, conserved on site, that bear high quality busts of the principal deities of Hierapolis, characterised by various symbols and attributes, within vegetal scrolls. Together with Artemis and Apollo, there is Selene with her lunar crescent,

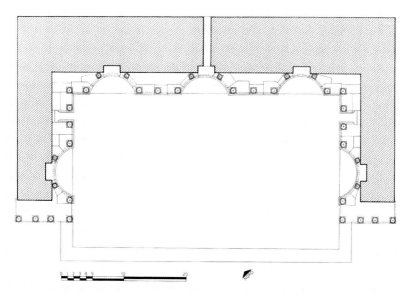

Fig. 114   Temple Nymphaeum: plan.

Fig. 115   Temple Nymphaeum: graphic reconstruction (D. De Bernardi Ferrero).

133

Jupiter represented as a local deity with a heavy woollen cloak, and Juno flanked by peacocks. The abundant decoration includes motifs tied to the world of water and nymphaea, such as Erotes riding sea monsters with refined snake-like tails within the coffers of the ceiling.

Other slabs, which have been found during the excavation of this monument, are housed in the Museum. They bear representations of the Amazonomachy and of standing deities (one clearly shows Apollo's tripod) and presumably decorated the parapet of the basin. Unfortunately, they have been severely corroded by gas exhalations from the bottom of the basin and from the cavities that may be found around the whole area of the Temple.

The construction of this building, strongly linked to the sacred area, belongs to a period during the third century that witnessed great transformations in the rather primitive layout of this most important civic cult site.

Fig. 116   Tympanum with the bust of Zeus, from the Temple Nymphaeum.

Fig. 117
Relief from the Temple
Nymphaeum with an Amazon.

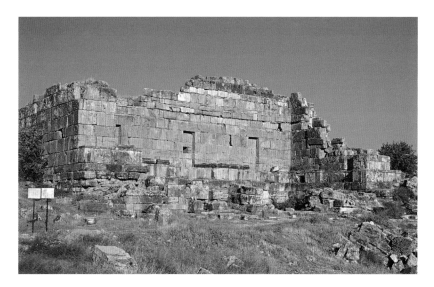

Fig. 118 The Temple Nymphaeum.

Behind the wall of the nymphaeum are the remains of the

Temple of Apollo [17]

The Temple, which may be recognised by its marble staircase, lies within a sacred area, about 70 metres long, which was surrounded by an enclosure wall *(temenos)*. The enclosure was in turn surrounded, at least on its southern, western and northern sides, by a marble portico which has been only partially excavated.

An elegant marble portico may be seen, with pilasters bearing fluted Doric semi-columns supporting capitals that are decorated below with a row of astragali and beads and which, on the echinus, bear a series of ovolos. Lying on the ground are fragments of the trabeation, bearing a refined Doric frieze with triglyphs, metopes and various rosettes, which were also repeated on the external, travertine, wall. The portico provided an elegant frame to the sacred area and was built towards the end of the first century AD during the great Flavian reconstruction following the disastrous Neronian earthquake. The plan of the Doric peribolos recalls the Domitianic one along the Street of Frontinus, and forms part of a more general architectural tendency which may be recognised in the façades along the monumental way to the *Sebasteion* at *Aphrodisias*, dated to late Julio-Claudian times, or in the travertine Doric façades of the nearby cities of *Tripolis*, *Blaundus* and *Laodicea*.

The structures of the Temple are later, though the presence of two beautiful Ionic capitals in the Museum (see under Museum), as well as of a Corinthian capital of the first century AD and other architectural fragments lead us to suppose the existence of an earlier temple on the site.

The sacred area lies on two terraces cut into the travertine bedrock, which were connected by a marble staircase. The temple

Fig. 119 Doric portico around the Temple of Apollo.

Fig. 120 Ionic capital from the Temple of Apollo.

Fig. 121 Fragment of a colossal statue of an Emperor, perhaps Hadrian, from the temple area.

on its podium lay in the south-eastern corner of the Doric peribo-los and occupied part of the marble staircase, on an oblique axis which was conditioned by both religious motivations and the presence of the underlying Plutonium grotto, only partly regular-ised by a travertine barrel-vault. We do not know whether or not, there was another building, besides the main temple, dedicated to deities such as Artemis, Leto or Hades, all strongly associated with the religious characteristics of this site.

Apart from the staircase, the temple of Apollo also survives in its podium with its marble revetment and cornice mouldings. The almost square plan of the cella may be seen, measuring 11.50 m wide and 10.20 m long, probably divided internally by two rows of columns, and with a façade with two wings that flanked the entrance with its pair of marble columns. The chronology may be deduced from the blocks, some bearing inscriptions, that are to be

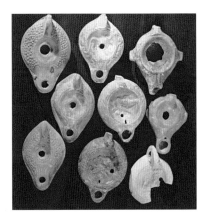

Fig. 122 Lamps from the temple area.   **Fig. 123** Fragments of relief-decorated glazed vases from the temple area.

found reused in the wings' capitals, in the cella wall and in the pavement. One of them bears incised the text of the famous alphabetic oracle that the faithful received in the sanctuary (see Appendix, p. 228). Thus the construction of the temple may be assigned to the third century AD, also on the basis of the decorative style of the architecture. This period corresponds to one of radical reconstruction of the complex, together with the erection of the nymphaeum.

On the staircase behind the temple is a late fill, containing pieces from the buildings of the sanctuary of Apollo after they had fallen out of use. They include columns, fragments of architraves, capitals and marble bases, as well as a high quality marble statue representing a draped woman, sculpted according to the statuary dictates of the fourth century BC. The accompanying inscription tells us that it was dedicated by Affia, daughter of Zeuxis, to the *Dei Augusti* (the emperors) and the *Demos* (the personification of the civic body of Hierapolis).

The whole area around the temple must have been adorned by statues. The marble fragments include other female figures, perhaps of priestesses, and part of a colossal statue of an emperor with a cuirass and the figure of a barbarian kneeling at his feet, probably representing Hadrian (fig. 121, see Museum below) on the basis of parallels with analogous statues from Crete and Olympia.

The excavations have brought to light numerous dumps of pottery in the area of the temple which are the remains of the votive offerings of the faithful. Hundreds of pieces of cups with red and brown slips and decorated in relief according to the Megarian ware tradition are proof of libation rites, whilst the numerous lamps, from the first century BC to the end of the first century AD, are presumably also linked to cult ceremonies, perhaps nocturnal, that took place within the sanctuary.

Two small marble stele were found along with the pottery. They bear dedications in Greek and the symbol of the double-axe that was linked to the cult of Apollo *Kareios* or *Karios*, from nearby Caria, which appellation reveals his oracular and, according to some scholars, also his chthonic character, further enhanced by the presence of the Plutonium and the subterranean phenomena that characterised him.

Fig. 124 Marble statue from the area of the temple.

Plutonium [18]

The discovery of the Plutonium during the 1962 to 1965 excavation seasons constitutes one of the most interesting results of Italian research at Hierapolis. It is a very suggestive place which, prior to its discovery, was known only through the description of the Greek geographer Strabo, who lived at the time of Augustus. In book XIII of his work he wrote that "below a small brow of the mountainous country that lies above it, is an opening of only moderate size, large enough to admit a man, but it reaches a considerable depth" (translation by H.L. Jones, *Loeb Ed.*). The writer, furthermore, documented a quadrangular enclosure in which vapours were so dense as to impede the sight of the ground. Bulls were brought there to be sacrificed through the exhalations. Strabo himself threw some sparrows into the Plutonium, recording their immediate death. Only the Galloì eunuchs, priests of Cybele, remained immune, perhaps, according to the geographer,

Fig. 125 Entrance to the Plutonium.

because of their particular malformation or because of the divine protection afforded to them as adepts of the sanctuary. In antiquity the place was considered to be one of the entrances to the Underworld, or *Ditis spiracula* (chinks of Dite, god of the Underworld), according to the definition of Apuleius, a Latin writer of the third century AD.

The opening to the Plutonium lies to the right of the Temple, along a natural travertine face which was cut back. Its entrance is crowned with a marble niche decorated with a shell motif. A circular *aedicula* that signalled the sacrality of the site was built on the rock platform above during the first century AD. The small marble structure, a sort of tholos, had an elegant decoration of floral scrolls on its podium (see Museum below).

The entrance to the Plutonium, from where it is possible to hear the gurgling underground waters, is now closed by a wall because of the danger of poisonous gases that accumulate towards the floor of the cavity and which, only a few years ago,

Fig. 126   Circular base with floral decoration.

led to the deaths of some incautious explorers. The thought can only recall the words of Strabo and is emphasised by the bodies of birds which are killed by the exhalations during the night, when they are attracted by the heat of the rock.

From the Temple of Apollo, in the direction of the theatre, we may recognise the structural remains of an insula which include

The "House of the Ionic Capitals" [19]

Along the secondary road *(stenopos)* that leads to the theatre is the façade of a house, facing south, that has been the object of excavations by an équipe of the University of Venice since 1989. The existence of varied construction techniques in the structure tell us that the block saw chronological phases and underwent a series of modifications.

The *domus*, a seigniorial house spreading out horizontally, is organised in various rooms that open onto a central square peristyle, with three columns per side, currently in course of restoration. The thin columns, 2.95 metres high, are in a reddish breccia marble with white marble Ionic capitals that have given the name to the house. The excavation of the rubble also revealed smaller columns in precious onyx, also with Ionic capitals, that suggest that the building possessed a second floor. The original structure, on the basis of the style

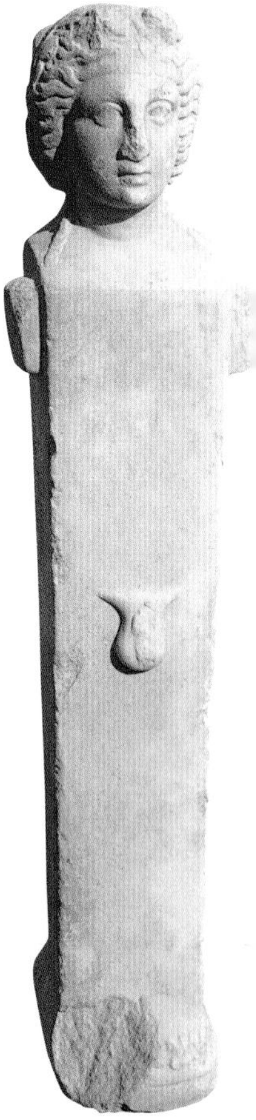

Fig. 127
House of the Ionic Capitals: Dionysian herm.

employed for the architectural elements, dates to the second century AD when the pavements where built of tile *opus spicatum*, according to the remains discovered in the western and eastern porticoes. The house must have belonged to one of the aristocratic families of the city, documented in particular during the times of the sophist Antipater, as is indicated by the discovery of numerous marble furnishings. They include a herm with the head of Dionysios, and the head of a bearded deity (Hercules or Zeus?), that may be considered a Roman copy of an original in the Greek severe style of the second quarter of the fifth century BC. The house must have been severely damaged during the earthquake of the fourth century AD, though it maintained its role as an aristocratic residence, even if radical restructuring brought about the closure of the southern portico of the peristyle. Thus a new room was created, with a sumptuous *opus sectile* pavement, using a variety of coloured marbles, including porphyry, with rectangles enclosing polygonal shapes. This room was a reception hall that opened onto a vestibule containing a bench for visitors who were waiting to be received by the *dominus*. His

Fig. 129   House of the Ionic Capitals: view of the courtyard.

seal ring was also discovered. In the eastern part of the insula, a dividing wall appears to define a new living area, sited at a higher level, following the slope of the hill. This area includes a large hall paved with tiles and smaller rooms, one of which was probably a kitchen.

Even these houses were destroyed by the earthquake of the first half of the seventh century, as is shown by the large rubble spreads beneath which have been found sixth century ceramics and coins of the emperor Justinian.

Between the tenth and eleventh centuries, poor Byzantine houses with walls built of limestone blocks and beaten earth floors were erected over the rubble, witnessing an ephemeral renewal prior to the final abandonment of the site.

After the "House of the Ionic capitals", we continue up the slope towards the imposing remains of the

Theatre [20]

The space between the houses and the large wall of the back-stage is occupied by blocks of marble coming from the decoration of the *scaenae frons* (architectural backdrop) of the theatre, which had collapsed onto the stage and into the orchestra, and which the Italian Archaeological Mission has brought to light during the long and involved work directed by Daria De Bernardi Ferrero. The straight and curved architrave blocks that belong to the three orders of the *scaenae frons*, characterised by sumptuous vegetal decoration of the friezes, are aligned on the left. Of note are the Greek letters incised on the ends of the blocks, intended to facilitate the complex positioning of the heavy pieces during the building's construction. Closer to the theatre are the architrave blocks of the first order which bear the monumental dedicatory inscription, whose text has been reconstructed by Tullia Ritti:

Text of the inscription incised on the architrave of the first order:

a) upper line

['Απόλλωνι 'Αρχηγέτη καὶ τοῖς θεο]ῖς ἄλλοις πατρίοι[ς καὶ]
Αὐτοκράτορσι [κυρίοις ἡμῶ]ν Λ(ουκίῳ) Σεπτιμίῳ Σεουήρῳ καὶ
Μ(άρκῳ) Αὐρ(ηλίῳ) 'Αντωνείνῳ [Σεβαστοῖς? καὶ Π(οπλίῳ) Σεπτιμίῳ
Γέτᾳ Καίσαρι] καὶ 'Ιουλίᾳ Δόμνῃ Σεβαστῇ μητρὶ κάστρων καὶ
τῷ σύνπαντι οἴκῳ αὐτῶν, ἡ λαμπροτάτη 'Ιεραπολειτῶν πόλις
ἐκ θεμελί[ων τὴν] πρώτην σκηνὴν τοῦ θ[ε]άτρου σὺν παντὶ τῷ
κόσμῳ κατεσκεύασεν [καὶ ἐσκού]τλωσεν ἐξ οἰκείων πόρων,
ἀνθυπατεύοντος Κ(οίντου) Τινηίου Σακέρδωτος, ταμίου δὲ καὶ
πρεσβ(ευτοῦ) καὶ ἀντιστρατήγου καὶ λογιστοῦ τῆς πόλεως

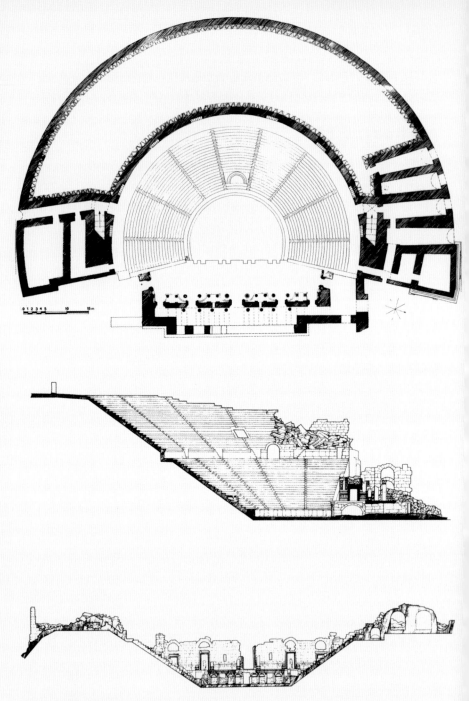

Fig. 130 Theatre: plan and sections.

[Μ(άρκου)] Οὐλπ(ίου) Δομιτίου ᾿Αρισταίου ᾿Αραβιανοῦ, ἐπιτρόπων δὲ τῶν Σεβ(αστῶν) Αἰ[λ(ίου) --ου] καὶ Αὐρ(ηλίου) ᾿Αριμνάστου, στρατηγούντων τῆς πόλεω[ς] τῶν περὶ Μόδεστον δὶς τοῦ [---]ωνος, ἐπι[μελ]ησαμένων Τ(ίτου) Φλ(αβίου) ᾿Αθηναγόρου Αἰλιανοῦ καὶ Δημητρίου Ζωσίμου πο(λιτευομένων).

b) lower line

Συνετέλεσεν δὲ καὶ πρὸς τὸν κόσμον τῆς τε πρώτης καὶ τῆς δευτέρας στέγης λίθου Δοκιμηνοῦ ἀπηρτισμένου [καὶ πρὸς? τὴν προ]σάρτησιν παρ᾽ ἑαυτῆς, πόδας ἑξακοσ[ίους πε]ντήκοντα τρεῖς, ἡ τέχνη τῶν πορφυραβά[φων].

Translation:

a) "To Apollo Archegetes and to the father gods and to [our lords ?] emperors L. Septimius Severus and M. Aurelius Antoninus [Augusti ?] and [P. Septimius Geta Caesar], and to Julia Domna Augusta, *mater Castrorum*, and to all their house, the splendid city of Hierapolis built from the foundations and covered with encrustations the first stage of the theatre with all its decoration, through its own finances, during the consulate of Q. Tineius Sacerdos, under the quaestor and *legatus pro praetore* and curator of the city M. Ulpius Domitius Aristaeus Arabianus, and procurators of the Augusti Aelius [---] and Aurelius Arimnastos, and being strategoi of the city Modestos, son of Modestos, of [---] and his colleagues, and being curators T. Flavius Athenagoras Aelianus and Demetrios Zosimos, citizen functionaries"

b) "the corporation of purple dyers also contributed towards the ornamentation of both the first and the second storey (lit. "soffit"), in worked Dokimion marble, and to that part added to it, for 653 feet"

We may now head towards the left side of the theatre, through a large entranceway surmounted by an arch that leads towards the centre of the building, along the route of the *diazoma*. To the right is a large wall of squared travertine blocks, corresponding to the back of the theatre's *scaenae frons*. Relieving arches may be seen within the structure. Whilst the southern half collapsed during the early Middle Ages (restorations are in progress), the northern half, that shows serious instability and a dangerous outwards leaning, was consolidated in 1992, thanks to a financial contribution by Fiat Corporation of Istanbul and the Koç Foundation. The wall was taken to pieces and then reconstructed, with the substitution of some of the more fragmented pieces, and the whole structure was then reinforced with inox steel cleats.

By entering the theatre along the *diazoma* we gain a superb vision of Hierapolis' principal monument, which has seen the work of excavation and restoration of Italian architects and archaeologists over a period of more than twenty years of continuous endeavour. The theatre is of impressive size and occupies four blocks, even though its orientation, instead of following the urban layout, takes advantage of the slope in the best Hellenistic tradition that was maintained in Roman Asia Minor, whilst in Italy, Africa and the western provinces the seats of the cavea were supported on artificial substructures with corridors and vaulted radial walls (see for instance the Theatre of Marcellus in Rome).

Nonetheless, the outer seats of the cavea at Hierapolis, because of the building's size, had to be sustained by horizontal or oblique barrel-vaulted galleries.

The steeply sloping cavea is divided into two parts by the central *diazoma* and is divided vertically by 8 staircases into 9 *cunei (kerkides)*, whilst one of the *cunei* of the *summa cavea* is further divided in two. Above was the gallery of the *summa cavea* built, according to a long inscription, in Hadrianic times. The seats differ: those of the lower rows and only one *cuneus* of the *summa cavea* are in marble, whilst the others are in travertine. In the centre of the *ima cavea* (the lower seats) is a large marble exedra or *proedria*, with seats having lion paw terminals and high backs, for persons of high rank and perhaps even emperors such as Caracalla whilst visiting the city. The *cavea* is divided from the

Fig. 131 Aerial view of the theatre.

orchestra by a high podium that was built in later times, perhaps during the fourth century AD when the orchestra was transformed into a pool *(colimbetra)* with the closure of the three central doors of the *hyposcenium*, the lining of the feature with hydraulic mortar and the construction of two small side staircases so as to descend into the water. Various aquatic representations were performed here, following a use attested in various cities of the Empire, provoking the condemnation of Christians and the invectives of St. John Chrysostom, thus creating further negative orientations against everything that the ancient and noble theatrical traditions represented.

On the right extremity of the podium, next to the stairs, was a slab dating to Severan times (the original is in the Museum), with an important relief representing the exaltation of the athletic contests, like the frieze over the central door of the *scaenae frons* (fig. 138). In the centre is probably the personification of Hierapolis who, as in the central relief of the *scaenae frons*, bears a statue of Apollo Archegetes, protector of the city, and at the same time is being crowned by the personification of Tyche (good fortune), represented with a horn of plenty and a towered crown. At her feet is the torrent *Chrysorhoas*, shown as a reclining old-man. To the left is another figure with a towered crown, perhaps *Oikoumene* (the land inhabited by men), effecting a libation over a lighted altar with a bull, the symbol of sacrifice, to one side. Behind is a cylindrical crown, symbol of the prize of the victors which, unlike the relief of the *scaena*, is decorated with scalloping instead of bosses.

The cavea is joined to the majestic stage building creating a unitary enclosed structure in the fashion of the models of Roman architecture. Only the wall of the first storey now survives. This

Fig. 132 Theatre: restoration of the back wall of the stage in 1992.

Fig. 133 Theatre: restoration of the stage building.

Fig. 134 View of the theatre.

supported two further storeys which height reached that of the *summa cavea*. This impressive building was erected in the third century AD, during the reign of the emperor Septimius Severus, both enveloping and cancelling earlier phases. We may hypothesise the existence of a theatre already in Flavian times judging from the reused architectural fragments that belonged to the *scaena*. To the same phase belongs a marble statue of a female figure with combed curls along her forehead, typical of the end of the first century AD (see under Museum, below).

The construction of the gallery of the *summa cavea*, with the rich marble decoration of its architraves and soffits, is to be assigned to Hadrianic times.

However, the building of the scaena with its splendid decoration in precious marbles which, from the inscription, come from

Fig. 135 Winter view of the theatre.

Phrygian quarries, particularly *Dokymeion*, dates to the time of Septimius Severus.

The inscription (see p. 147) dedicates the building to Apollo, to the gods of the city, to the Emperor Septimius Severus, to his wife Julia Domna and to their sons Caracalla and Geta (the name of the latter was erased from the inscription through the *damnatio memoriae* ordered by his brother). Links between Hierapolis and the Imperial Court in Rome were very strong at this time. Indeed, Antipater, a philosopher of the New Sophistry and citizen of Hierapolis, had great influence in the capital, both as tutor to the princes Caracalla and Geta and as chief chancellor responsible for relationships with the Greek cities. It is probable that alongside the local finances, contributed by the purple dyers for example,

Fig. 136   Work in progress on the casts of the theatre reliefs.

the Emperor himself helped to realise the ambitious and expensive project through the intercession of Antipater.

The stage building is divided into a *logeion* (the stage itself) and a *scaena* with a large backdrop. The *logeion* was badly damaged by the collapse of the backdrop and has been largely restored with the reconstruction of the arches in travertine blocks which supported the stage floor built with slabs of limestone. This has been partly reconstructed using concrete covered with powdered travertine so as to blend with the surrounding colours. Even the structure of the proscenium has been reconstructed with original pieces discovered in the rubble, with limited integration of gaps with white concrete and marble powder. Thus has a precious document of third century Roman architecture been recovered.

The *logeion* has a height of little more than three metres and thus preserves the proportions of the Greek and not of the Roman stage which, according to Vitruvius, should have been lower. Its façade is articulated with niches and five doors within the wall. A row of spiral fluted columns with composite capitals sustains an articulated marble trabeation, which emerges in correspondence with the doors and re-enters with the niches, thus creating a dynamic plastic effect, full of suggestion, emphasised by the dense decorative interlace of the frieze with scrolls that include rosettes and that terminates in the centre with elegant scalloped motifs. Within the niches, with calottes in the form of seashells, are various figures including peacocks, wild beasts with serpentine bodies and crowns.

The *scaena* with its rich decoration was unearthed during the excavation of the earth and blocks of collapsed rubble that covered the entire building, from the architraves of the side doors, to the orchestra and the first fourteen rows of seats in the cavea.

Fig. 137 Stage with reliefs of Apollo and Artemis.

Fig. 138 Relief in the orchestra showing the celebration of the games.

Fig. 139   Frieze from the theatre with masks and garlands.

An extraordinary example of micro-Asiatic architecture has now emerged. The *scaenae frons* was articulated in three superimposed orders and, according to the tradition of Asia Minor, had 5 doors, instead of the 3 doors that characterise the western theatres, and two entrances to the *paraskenia* (wings to the sides of the stage). The door jambs, architraves and frames of these doors all present minute decoration characterised by a *horror vacui* which the presence of smooth listels helps to emphasise. The use of a drill on the marble surfaces creates chromatic contrasts such that the worked stone begins to resemble lace. The effect is further accentuated by figures inserted into the acanthus scrolls that occupy some of the larger surfaces, including animals, birds, erotes fighting lions and even deities such as Nemesis, who appears on the jamb of the left side door.

Fig. 140 Decorated block from the soffit of the *scaenae* frons.

On the left hand side of the *scaena*, in a less visible position in the pilasters abutting the wall above the podium, the various phases of work in the decoration may be seen. At times the work seems to have been interrupted at various stages: the outlining of motifs with a scalpel, the use of a drill with holes that define the decorative details, the exportation of the thin diaphragms between the drill holes and the final finishings.

The three orders of the *scaenae frons*, supported by monolithic marble columns, sit upon a podium that runs around the three sides, interrupted by exedras in correspondence with the main doors. They have cornices decorated with acanthus and oak leaves and bear a very interesting figurative cycle dedicated to Apollo and Artemis that unfolds along the 47 blocks. This is quite singular insofar as most Roman theatres have Dionysian themes.

The figured slabs found in position have been left there, whilst those discovered in fragments in the collapsed rubble have been restored and substituted with copies, the originals being housed in the Museum. The reliefs present a narrative through images of the myths tied to the two most important deities at Hierapolis and, indeed, in the whole of Asia Minor. Beginning at the central exedra, the right hand side is dedicated to the Apollo cycle, whilst the left recounts that of Artemis.

The Apollo Cycle (Fig.s 142 a-b)

This begins with the scene of the hierogamy (the sacred wedding) of Zeus seated on a throne, touching the shoulder of Leto (1); this is followed by the birth of Apollo (2), with Leto reclining on a bed and the maids washing the child (this is the same scheme later used to represent the birth of Christ), and then by the god's infancy, when he is being trained in hunting and fighting (3). The straight side of the podium bears a rare representation of the death of Adonis, the handsome youth loved by Aphrodite and punished by Apollo (4). To the left the god is performing a victory libation on a lit altar. There is also a rare illustration of the veiled Aphrodite with the naked body of the youth on her knees, an extraordinary anticipation of Piety common to Christian art. To the side is Apollo on a chariot led by griffins attacking a giant whose extremities assume the form of a serpent (5). As in the Pergamum frieze, he is vainly defended by mother Gea, the earth, who emerges from the ground and extends her hand in supplication towards the god. The feats of Apollo continue in the side exedra, which presents a myth strongly linked to this part of Asia Minor, that of Marsyas, the Silenus venerated in the nearby Phrygian city of Kelainai, besides which developed Apamea on the Meander.

Fig. 141   Stage front.

1   2   3

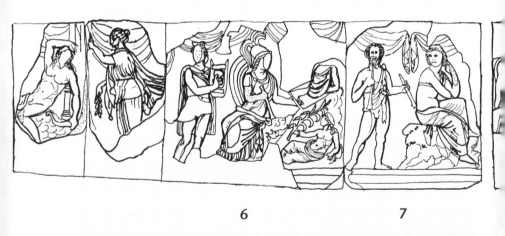

6   7

Fig. 142 a   Theatre: graphic reconstruction of the Apollo frieze.

4

5

9

10

11   12

15

Fig. 142 b Theatre: graphic reconstruction of the Apollo frieze.

13   14

16

165

Fig. 143   Relief with the birth of Apollo.

The tale opens with Athena seated next to a spring who, on seeing her face deformed by its reflection in the water whilst she was playing the flutes, throws away the musical instrument which is picked-up by Marsyas (6). The Silenus then challenges Apollo to a musical contest for which *hybris* he is duly punished (7). He is dragged away bound by the executioner whilst the youth Olympos prays Apollo to spare his tutor (8). The scene in which Marsyas is bound to a pine-tree and flayed alive is one of the most interesting as it presents the motive of the hung Silenus which was reproduced by numerous Roman copyists (9). Even the figure sharpening his knife is the exact reproduction of the famous statue of the so-called "Arrotino" (Knife-grinder), now in the Uffizi Gallery in Florence. The Hierapolitan frieze with the naked figure of Apollo who watches the scene impassive with his arms crossed

Fig. 144
Relief with the
birth of Artemis.

Fig. 145   The death of Adonis.

Fig. 146 The suffering of Marsyas.

reproduces a famous Hellenistic statuary group that archaeologists have assigned to Pergamum. The Marsyas cycle concludes
with the apotheosis of Apollo crowned by the nymphs (10). Here
again he is naked, seated on a rock and leaning on his quiver,
with his head poised on his right arm. The reference to statues of
Apollo Delphinios, the god of Greek colonists particularly venerated at Miletus in this guise, is evident.

The flat side presents Apollo as the god of purification, whilst
sprinkling water with a laurel branch (11). This is the god *kath-
arsios*, invoked by inscriptions to protect the city from pestilence.
In front of him is a lovely representation of dancing maidens who
hold themselves together with garlands (12). This tied dance is

Fig. 147 a-b   The incoronation of Apollo.

Fig. 148   Apollo the purifier with dancing maidens.

Fig. 149
Dancing Muses.

also linked to purification rites and evokes the cathartic function of Apollo during epidemics that struck the city. The representations on this side terminate with Apollo wearing his lengthy chiton (13), identified as the god Musagetes conducting the chorus of the Muses, depicted whilst dancing on the flat lateral wall to the sides of the door. At the angle stands the figure of a shepherd who appears ecstatic (14), perhaps because he is spellbound by the singing of the Muses who are shown with an accentuated dance movement quite different to the usual iconography of the standing Muses (15). As in a wall painting found in a house at Ephesus, a tenth Muse, Sappho, is depicted whilst holding a scroll that clearly refers to the verses composed by the famous Greek poetess. The cycle ends on the right-hand extremity with a standing figure holding a rudder and wearing a crown with towers (16). This is the personification of the Tyche (the Fortune) of Hierapolis.

The Artemis Cycle (Fig.s 150 a-b)

Returning to the centre, to the left of the central door is the cycle of Artemis beginning with the scene of her birth, both symmetrical and similar to the one of Apollo (1: fig. 144). This is followed by the infancy of the goddess who is playing on the knees of her father Zeus (2), seated upon a throne, in the presence of the *Horai* (the Four Seasons). The sculptor obviously wanted to depict the text of the hymn of Artemis by the Alexandrian poet Callimacus.

On the straight side is Artemis the hunter on a chariot drawn by deer and with her prey, a wild boar, lying at her feet, whilst her dog scratches his ear with his paw (3). On the left-hand side exedra, placed symmetrically to that of Marsyas, is another example of punished *hybris*, that of Niobe who dared to glorify the beauty of her twelve children above the divine offspring of Leto (4). The repercussions were terrible, as the wrath of the gods fired at the poor children, who are depicted escaping or struck down by arrows. On the left extremity Niobe tries in vain to protect her youngest child. Even this character is linked to the traditions of Asia, and an image of Niobe transformed into stone by the gods, taking pity on her lamentations, was displayed near *Magnesia*, along the Hermos valley (modern Manisa).

2   1

4

Fig. 150 a   Theatre: graphic reconstruction of the Artemis frieze.

3

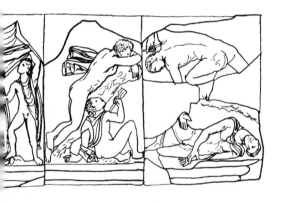

5

6

Fig. 150 b Theatre: graphic reconstruction of the Artemis frieze.

8   7

Fig. 151   The girl Artemis on the knees of Jupiter.

The continuance of the frieze has a radical change of theme: Artemis is no longer the deity of classical tradition, but is presented through the image of the Anatolian goddess worshipped in the great sanctuary at Ephesus. Even the direction of the scene changes, as on the following blocks up to the straight side, next to the door to the *paraskenion*, there is a procession in honour of the Ephesian deity, who is depicted both at the beginning and at the end of the procession, in front of a temple that contains her *simulacrum* (5). A priest carries out ritual libations, whilst the adepts sacrifice the bull and other temple adepts play flutes so as to calm and distract the animal at the moment of its slaughter (6).

Fig. 152   Artemis hunting.

Fig. 153
The killing of the
daughters of Niobe.

177

Fig. 154 Artemis kills the daughters of Niobe.

The long procession is formed of servants who lead the bulls, and others who carry garlands and offerings of fruit (5). It probably represents the annual procession that moved from Ephesus, along the sacred way, to the famous suburban sanctuary.

The two images of Artemis refer to the idol of the temple covered with precious metals as well as to the marble copy venerated in the city. The Hierapolis frieze has helped demolish one of the most widely held beliefs that the cult of Ephesus did not include blood sacrifice, as well as confirming the hypothesis of a Swiss archaeologist, G. Seiterle, regarding the so-called *polimastia* (many breasts) of the sacred idol. The *polimastia* is, in fact, a late interpretation by the Fathers of the Church who wanted to discredit the cult. The necklace present on the bust of the images of Artemis was made of the testicles of the sacrificed bulls that

Fig. 155 Sacrificial procession in honour of Artemis of Ephesus.

Fig. 156 The sacrifice of the bull.

were offered as the element that most effectively symbolised fertility, recalling ancient Anatolian propitiatory rites. Indeed, even other, male, cult statues, such as those of Zeus Labraundeus, the main deity of Caria who was worshipped near Mylasa with the two-edged axe, wear pectorals similar to those of Artemis.

The cycle concludes with the images of divinities that are linked to themes of athletic contest: Dike (Justice) with her scales (7), and Nemesis (8), the goddess of just prizes to victors, in the propitiatory act of spitting on her breast.

The cycles of Apollo and Artemis are part of a more complex iconographic programme that is developed in the three orders of the *scaenae frons* through other friezes and the statues that were housed in the niches. The blocks of the first order celebrate Dionysian themes as well as those linked to the Plutonium: the rape of Proserpine and the search for her daughter by Demetra on her dragon-drawn chariot (fig. 202). The frieze above the central door *(porta regia)* develops another theme that is closely linked to the theatre, that of the civic games, the Apolloneia Pythia Oikoumenika, with their glorification in the presence of Septimius Severus and the Imperial family, in front of the symbolic metal crown of cylindrical form with bosses, which was the prize for the victors (fig. 199). To the sides are images of personifications linked to the games (see Museum). Even the numerous statues in the niches represent the themes of Hierapolitan religion with Artemis, Apollo Kareios, Leto depicted in the form of an elegantly clad nymph leaning on a small pillar (fig. 205-206), and last but not least Hades, god of the underworld, seated on a throne to the side of which is the dog Cerberus, recalling his world which was made manifest by the exhalations of the nearby Plutonium (fig. 207).

Two larger than life statues of deities or female personifications are located in front of the side doors. That to the right holds a sceptre and bears knotted ribbons that drop down the sides of her face, whilst the other, now headless, is characterised by a harmonious drapery that derives from Pergamene models of Hellenistic date. The former could represent *Oikoumene*, whilst the latter might be the personification of Tragedy.

The theatre continued to be used into late Roman times, when an inscription was incised on the lower band of the second order architrave. Dating to AD 352, it records the restoration of the *scaenae frons* which was falling to ruin. Indeed, behind the wall that supports the architectural decoration of the *scaenae frons* are some large "breccia" columns that served to sustain the structure that, in turn, bore the substantial weight of the three superimposed orders of colonnades. There must also have been a number of modifications during the fifth and sixth centuries, when the building appears to have lost its theatrical function. The doors of the *scaenae frons* were transformed into narrow passages with the construction of walls composed of antique reused masonry. One of these walls even contained the block depicting the birth of Artemis. Rather poor houses were inserted into the sumptuous Severan architecture. Testimony to this late phase of occupation are the inscriptions with Christian symbols in the upper part of the blocks of the *proskenion* (colonnade in front of the stage or skene). The great earthquake at the beginning of the seventh century didn't spare the large marble *scaenae frons*, which collapsed precipitously into the orchestra, and which has been brought to light through the excavations of the last few decades.

Climbing up the gallery of the summa cavea, not without having admired the landscape of the Lykos Valley with the mass of the Baba Dağ (mount Salbakos) that dominates the plain in front of us, we can visit

The Church Above the Theatre (21)

This is a hypostile church with a nave, two aisles and a single apse. The Ionic capitals with impost blocks are similar to those of the cathedral. The columns were substituted with pillars in a secondary phase, whilst at a later date, probably during the middle ages, the church was reduced to its single nave, whilst the aisles were transformed into houses through the construction of dividing walls. Many graves are to be seen dug through the pavement. The second century sarcophagus with busts depicting a deceased couple within garlands held by funerary Erotes (see Museum, p. 214) was found in this building, reused as a basin.

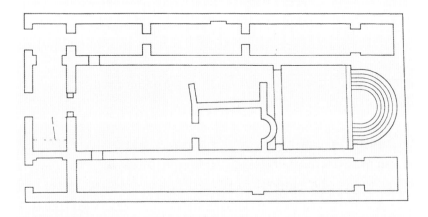

Fig. 157 General plan of the church.

Climbing the slope between the remains of houses, after having passed through the line of the proto-Byzantine fortifications (early fifth century AD), an imposing structure meets our eyes:

The Castellum Aquae (22)

Drinkable water was guaranteed to the city by means of two aqueducts that were formed of simple channels on the slopes of the surrounding hills, now only partly covered with stone slabs, which may still be recognised to the north between Pamukkale and Karahayıt, and to the east towards Güzel Pinar. The channels flowed into the *castellum aquae*, a large water-tower or reservoir from which departed clay pipes that distributed the water to various parts of the city by following the road system.

The building is very well preserved, and displays ashlar faces on an extending base with a square profile. As in almost all the other buildings at Hierapolis, holes cut in Medieval times to extract metal cleats, both iron and lead, may be seen at the

Fig. 158 Water reservoir (*castellum aquae*).

junctures of the stone blocks. The podium that contains the cistern has a double crowning with simple jutting mouldings that remind us of the funerary monuments in the cemeteries. The structure is to be dated to the moment of the town's maximum development, in the second century AD.

Upon crossing the valley, littered with tombs and sarcophagi, northwards, we reach a slope which bears a staircase that led to the most important cult building of Christian times:

The Octagonal Martyrion [23]

The building stands on a high plateau, within a cemetery area, from which it dominates the town and the surrounding landscape up to mount Honaz Dağ (Mt. Kadmos). It may be entered from the western edge of the plateau, where the bases of pillars that once sustained a portico in front of the façade are to be seen. We enter through a square room flanked by niches, with small columns and marble cornices that framed fountains for ablutions in the central octagonal room. This was the fulcrum of the entire building that Paolo Verzone dated to the end of the fourth or beginning of the fifth century, stating that it was "the work of a great architect, quite probably part of a specific court équipe ... For a sanctuary of such importance for the State religion and of so much prestige for the Empire", "apart from the necessary subsidies, even the project" must have come from the court of Constantinople. The construction of the building was realised by local craftsmen who, for centuries, had mastered the technique of building with travertine. The practise of sending out projects from the capital of the Empire is documented in the Life of Porphyrius, bishop of Gaza, written by Mark the Deacon. For the church built on the site of the Marneion, an antique pagan sanctuary, the Empress

Fig. 159 The Martyrion of St. Philip: aerial view.

Eudoxia had first sent the project and later the columns, with orders that they should be erected according to plan.

The martyrion is composed of a central octagonal room, of which the large stone piers survive. Eight rectangular rooms open onto the central octagon, each with three arches supported at their extremities by travertine piers and, in the centre, by marble columns on octagonal plinths. The number eight, which lies at the base of the entire architectural geometry of the structure, according to the Church Fathers such as Ambrose and Augustine, has a strong symbolic significance, passed down from classical antiquity (e.g. the Pythagoric ogdoade). The baptismal fonts are also octagonal, evoking eternal life and resurrection. The capitals, which bear limestone impost blocks, are also of marble and are of

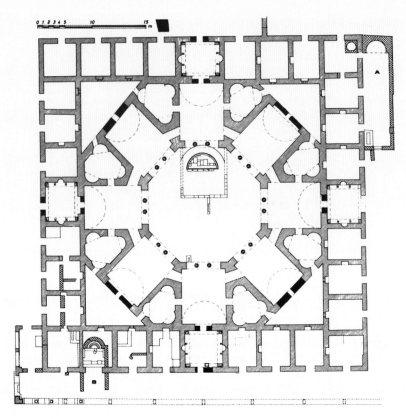

Fig. 160 Plan of the martyrion.

Fig. 161
Model of the
martyrion
(by P. Verzone).

Fig. 162
Martyrion: Arches
around the central
octagonal hall.

Fig. 163   Martyrion: Fountain niches in the entrance halls.

composite type with schematic acanthus leaves below small volutes that enclose a row of simply designed ovolos (fig. 166).

The piers are backed by transverse corridors built into the travertine walls like the Baths-Basilica (2), and have barrel-vaults and arches that bear Christian symbols within circles on their faces, including a cross within a star and a *chrismon* with an A and an Ω, the symbol of the beginning and end of everything. The central room, which contains a *synthronon* in the area of the altar, is paved with marble slabs, whilst the radial rooms bear mosaic pavements with large mosaic tesserae forming four-leafed geometrical motifs and a large braid and vegetal border scrolls.

The building was capped by a wooden dome covered with lead sheets that was destroyed in a fire. The excavations revealed large pieces of carbonised wooden beams and fragments of partially melted lead, whilst large areas of the walls around the central room are reddened by the fire. In some cases the travertine blocks have split under the heat. Between each of the rectangular rooms are curiously-shaped rooms with seven sides, three of which are apsed perhaps because they served as internal chapels. These rooms are connected to triangular courtyards, thus creating a square which circumscribes the complex church plan. The whole is, in turn, surrounded by 32 rooms aligned along the four sides of the square, with openings to the outside and beaten earth floors. The construction technique of the walls of these peripheral rooms consists of horizontal rows of small stones alternating with tile courses, with the rear walls perforated by tile-backed niches with barrel-vaults. A long rectangular chapel with a single apse, perhaps funerary, was later added to the southern side of the building. On the western side, to the left of the entrance, another apsed chapel was built within one of the small perimeter rooms after

Fig. 164
Bronze reliquary cross.
Sixth century AD.

Fig. 165 Martyrion: Christian symbols on the arches.

the destruction of the complex, perhaps caused by the seventh century earthquake. This was the last adjunct to recall the religious nature of the site.

This square building complex, typical of martyria, was erected within a funerary area and has been plausibly linked to the tradition of Philip the Deacon who, in Apostolic times, came to Hierapolis from Jerusalem and Caesarea with his four prophetic daughters. The homonym with the Apostle lies at the base of both the fusion between the two people and the legend, recounted in the *Acta Philippi*, of his fight, with the help of John the Apostle, with the Viper, the infernal deity that dominated the city. The octagonal building, that must have held the earthly remains of the Saint, recalls, both for its religious importance and its complex architecture, the Church of St. John, erected at Ephesus by Justinian over the tomb of the Saint. Thus, the two buildings celebrate the cult of the two protector Saints of Christianity in Asia Minor.

Fig. 166
Martyrion: marble capital of composite type, from the central octagonal room.

190

From the octagon we move northwards, along the uneven slope, where we can see the sepulchres of the:

Eastern Necropolis (24)

This part of the necropolis has the particular characteristics of a picturesque layout on the flank of a hill, where the monumental tombs appear aligned in formation in superimposed rows. They are of a very simple type, with a funerary chamber leaning against the rocky slope, which further appears to have been regularised through a series of cuts. Their roofs are formed of barrel vaults, masked with an exterior double-gable. In front of the façades are various travertine sarcophagi with inscriptions that, on epigraphic characteristics, appear even later, perhaps dating to the fourth century AD.

The layout of the funerary buildings and the cutting back of the rock in the eastern necropolis recall the cave-tombs found, for

Fig. 167   Eastern necropolis: tombs on the slope.

example, in Lycia, where even the tomb façades are sculpted in the rock. The tombs are distributed on the slope right down to the level of the Agora. At the foot of the slope, along the edges of the channel that borders the Byzantine walls, the tombs, some of which are in very good condition, are once again of the *heroon* type, with buildings consisting of a basement supporting the sarcophagi.

On returning to the Martyrion and the theatre, we descend towards the square of the Pamukkale Hotel, in the area of the ancient town centre, where lie the imposing ruins of the

Large Baths [25]

The great bathing complex, in which rooms is now housed the Archaeological Museum of Pamukkale, lies in the south-western part of the settlement, near the edge of the plateau that overlooks the travertine cascades. It was built in the second century AD during the revival that the city witnessed after the Neronian earthquake of AD 60, so as to exploit one of its principal resources, the spring water that still flows past the ruins of the Baths before gushing downhill.

The Baths represent the masterwork of local craftsmanship, showing off the capability in working the travertine stone that abounds throughout the region. The uncontrolled waters have deposited an imposing mass of limestone that covers the original pavements for a height of some four metres. Thus the soaring form of the architecture, consisting of two large halls where the barrel vaults are preserved and other rooms that have recently been restored, is no longer perceivable.

The series of rooms dedicated to the Museum corresponds to the halls that were heated in antiquity through the use of hypocausts. The Turkish General Directorate of Antiquities is presently committed to the excavation and restoration of the complex with the aim of bringing to light the original floor levels of these halls. In particular, the excavations have uncovered various late phases of occupation dating to medieval times, when the Roman spaces were transformed and subdivided with the construction of walls and the creation of small roads that give the idea of how, between the tenth and the thirteenth century, the bathing complex came to form the heart and centre of power of the settlement system that

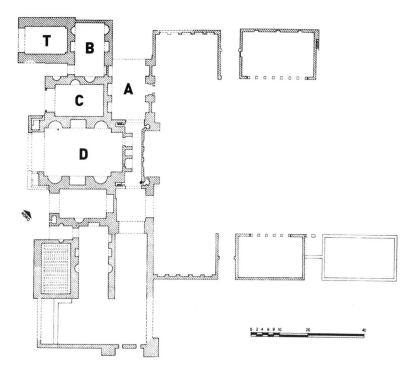

Fig. 168 General plan of the baths.

Fig. 169   Aerial view of the large baths.

Fig. 170   The baths and the palaestra in a photograph of the late 1950's.

replaced the ancient town. Even the discovery of beautiful glazed pottery of Byzantine and Seljuk date, much of which was imported, give an idea of the relative wealth of the people who occupied the ancient baths.

Within the baths we may see halls with large barrel-vaults, one with ribbing, already recorded by Choisy at the end of the nineteenth century. In hall T, the recent excavations have brought to light, on its western side, a singular apsed wall broken by three large windows framed by cornice mouldings. Usually the side walls of the halls have large rectangular or semicircular exedras, articulating the internal spaces following typical Roman architectural solutions. They held the marble statues that decorated these buildings in which the prestige of Roman power was displayed to all its glory.

Fig. 171 The large arches in the main hall of the baths.

Fig. 172   View of the baths and of the Lykos valley.

The main hall (D), measuring 20 x 32 metres, presents three exedras along its long sides, a square one between two semicircular ones, all with calottes bearing sumptuous stucco decoration in which we can still make out volutes with flowers and leaves bordering the large central shell. The walls must have been revetted with thin polychrome marble slabs fixed to the travertine walls with metal nails and cleats which have left holes in the structure. The two piers at the entrance have doors and an arched embrasure that let on to internal stairs that led up to the building's roofs. The large space to the east of the structure was occupied by a *palaestra* or site of athletic games. A series of large rectangular rooms with pilaster decorated walls in white and red stained "breccia" let onto this area.

From the baths we cross the asphalt square in the direction of the edge of the plateau and the travertine cascades, to reach the ruins of the medieval castle, once partially occupied by a modern hotel now, thankfully, demolished.

Medieval Castle [26]

This important monument, belonging to the last phases of life at Hierapolis, has become the subject of research only since 1994.

It is composed of a large enclosure wall that fortifies a tongue of the plateau, strategically placed so as to control the valley below. The wall is composed of reused material gathered from the ruined city, including various blocks of marble, some of which bear inscriptions. To the east is a door now suffocated by the calcareous channels. The upper part of the wall bears crenellations, blocked in a later phase, whilst on its inside, despite large cracks,

Fig. 173   The walls and towers of the medieval castle.

the battlements' walk and access stairs may still be seen. The castle also has a series of square towers.

Excavations carried out in one of the towers have brought to light the internal structure housing embrasures with pointed arches, the doorway and a pavement, as well as large cracks caused by an earthquake. The finds have allowed us to date the castle to between the eleventh and fourteenth century, when the area was fought over by Byzantines and Seljuk Turks, and a coin, representing the latter, was found in a layer of collapsed rubble.

From the Castle we return to the main street or plateia *where, to the south, stands another important Christian monument:*

The Church with Piers [27]

From an inscription we know that it was built by a priest, Kyriakos, who lived at the time of Bishop Gennadius, perhaps in the years after AD 535 when Hierapolis was elevated to the rank of metropolis of *Phrygia Pacatiana secunda*, thus sharing the dignity with nearby *Laodicea*.

There has been no systematic work on this building apart from the excavation of a series of trenches to locate the original level of the pavement. This church presents new architectural solutions when compared to the other Christian buildings of the city, emphasising the creative vivacity of the architects and craftsmen working at Hierapolis, who knew how to exploit to the full the possibilities offered by the travertine quarries.

The building, with a nave and two aisles, is preceded by a portico with piers. The apse is flanked by two rooms, the *prothesis* and the *diakonikon*, the latter serving as a sacristy. A noteworthy

Fig. 174   Plan of the Church with Piers.

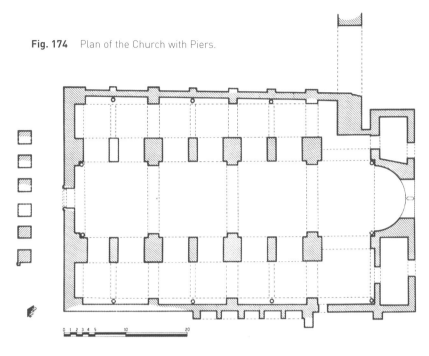

Fig. 175   The Church with Piers: the theatre may be seen in the background.

peculiarity is the use of piers of different sizes that divide the nave from the aisles, thus substituting the colonnades that we have seen in the other churches, including the Cathedral. The invention of this type of construction undoubtedly springs from a consolidated local technical tradition already attested in Roman times, in particular in the large bath building. The links with western architecture, as well as an anticipation of solutions that are to be found in Romanesque architecture, were emphasised by Paolo Verzone. The piers divide the central space into four bays, and the absence of small intermediate piers in the bay corresponding to the presbytery alludes to the presence of a pseudo-transept. In correspondence with the piers, along the perimeter walls are a series of pilasters and columns that introduce significant variations in the architectural forms, creating a series of vaulted ceilings of different sizes, according to whether they covered the nave or the aisles. The nave probably bore three barrel vaults, whilst the aisles may have borne cross-vaults. The western external wall reproduces the alternation of large and small pilasters, of different alternating widths, upon which were set a series of blind-arches.

Fig. 176   Remains of structures in the area of the gymnasium.

Returning to the line of the plateia, in a southerly direction, to the right, before the Byzantine gate, are the ruins of a building which can just be made out amongst the stones and vegetation:

The Gymnasium [28]

No excavations have been conducted in this area. However, it is possible to see an alignment of columns and an inscription which mentions the gymnasium. It must have comprised a large courtyard surrounded by a Doric portico. The architectural style allows us to include the building within the context of first century architecture at Hierapolis, probably dating to the same phase of post-earthquake rebuilding that is attested at the Temple of Apollo and along the Frontinus Street.

There are no traces of a Hellenistic gymnasium, and only archaeological excavation might reveal information about the earlier phases of what was undoubtedly one of the most important buildings for the civil and cultural life of the city.

After the gymnasium we come across the fortifications and

The Southern Byzantine Gate [29]

This opens onto the hills that drop down towards the Lykos valley, right in front of the mass of the *Honaz Dağ* (Mount *Kadmos*) that, especially at sunset, lights up in various shades of azure. In the last few years the Turkish General Directorate of Antiquities has completed a programme of reorganisation of the area, including the excavation and restoration of the southern Byzantine gate. This appears perfectly symmetrical, on the southern side of the town, to the gate that we have visited to the north and, like the latter, is to be dated to the end of the fourth century AD. It is built of travertine blocks and reused masonry, some in marble, and is flanked by two square towers. Like the other gate, it is

Fig. 177 The Byzantine south gate.

characterised by a large relieving arch placed above a monolithic architrave. However, the actual height of the door is somewhat lower than its twin. The recent work has brought about the removal of collapsed masonry and has integrated ample portions of the wall. Many interesting marble fragments with inscriptions have come to light. One of these joins with an inscription from the commercial Agora and provides proof that the wall was built in a single moment, using mainly blocks from the Agora, transported to the other side of the city on carts along the large *plateia*.

Because of the steeper slope, on this side of the site the calcareous depositions are even more marked than to the north, covering the route of a road lined with buildings bearing Doric façades, as in the Frontinus Street, that leads to the:

Southern Frontinus Gate? [30]

On the southern side of the city there is an urban organisation which appears exactly symmetrical to that created by Frontinus on the northern side, so much so that it would seem that it was all part of a single building phase wanted by the same people. The problem may be resolved only with the discovery of fragments of the dedicatory inscription. At the present state of work, which has been rendered particularly difficult due to the thick calcareous overburden that covers the building almost up to the springing of the arches, we can see the entranceway formed of three doors, roofed with vaults, and flanked by two towers. Unlike the northern gate, these are square in plan. In the area there are various fragments of marble deriving from an attic.

Fig. 178 The southern entrance to the archaeological area.

Fig. 179 View of the southern necropolis.

The systemisation of the area around the southern entrance, with its tourist reception centre covered with a large steel roof as at the northern entrance, has allowed the discovery and excavation of various buildings belonging to the:

Southern Necropolis [31]

To the right of the large roof, there is impressive evidence of seismic activity. An enormous block of natural travertine has been totally overturned and on its ancient ground level there may be seen traces of quarrying and rectangular graves that are attributable to a very simple, and perhaps earlier, cemetery.

During the excavations, carried out by the équipe of the Museum of Denizli during the reorganisation of the area, a travertine *bomòs* building with its long inscription, now laid out close by, was brought to light. Nearby is another tumulus of late Hellenistic date, to the side of which were found some important marble stelae with inscriptions.

New excavations are also being carried out on the northern side of the area, at the foot of the slope upon which rises the Byzantine wall circuit. The funerary structures, which have also yielded some noteworthy figured marble sarcophagi, had, above a base in stone blocks, walls built of small irregular stones with a roof of wooden beams covered with tiles. This type of structure is a novelty also for the polychrome wall-paintings that decorated the interior.

To the south, past the southern gate which is perhaps attributable to Frontinus and along the road that led to *Laodicea* and *Colossae*, are other funerary buildings.

Of particular interest is the tomb of Tiberius Claudius Talamus, cited in its lengthy inscription. The façade reproduces that of a house and recalls the architecture along the Frontinus Street with its square sectioned Doric pilasters and engaged columns alternating with windows bearing stone grates which, as at *Blaundus*, bear an Ionic trabeation with an architrave, a frieze bearing the inscription, and a cornice with dentils. In the buildings along the Street of Frontinus, however, the Doric order is also coherently developed in the capitals and in the trabeation with its frieze of metopes and triglyphs.

Fig. 180   Museum: garland decorated sarcophagus from the region of Denizli.

Archaeological Museum [32]

The Archaeological Museum was inaugurated in 1984. In the vast rooms of the ancient Roman baths it gathers together finds from the Vilayet (province) of Denizli, which were originally housed in a house in Denizli itself that is now an Ethnographic Museum.

Most of the objects exhibited are of Hellenistic and Roman date and come from Hierapolis. Prehistory is, nonetheless, represented by the conspicuous assemblage from Beycesultan, whilst finds from *Laodicea, Colossae, Tripolis, Attuda* and *Thiounta*, represent the Classical period. The entrance, from the north, leads to an ample courtyard, enlivened by the passage of a thermal water channel and by a garden in which various architectural fragments and funerary stelae, with figures and inscriptions referring to the deceased and their family, coming from the territory, are displayed.

Fig. 181   Museum: funerary stele with banquet scene from the region of Denizli.

Fig. 183 Museum: fragment of draped statue.

Fig. 182 Museum: votive stele of Zeus from the region of Denizli.

Fig. 184
Museum: bust of
a nude male statue.

In the open room in front of hall A are various marble statues. To the right is the bust of a nude male figure and the statue of a seated philosopher. At the back, in front of a glass dividing wall, are blocks from the circular structure found in the area of the Plutonium, upon which may be seen the traces of a colonnade. The frieze bears vegetal volutes datable to the first century AD. On the left is an alignment of sarcophagi from the necropolis of the city, dating to the second and third centuries AD. The largest is of Sidamara type, which niches containing various figures and is framed by columns. At the centre is the representation of the deceased dressed as a philosopher. The doors of the sepulchre, in front of which is a circular altar with a flame, are on the short sides. The lid bears the reclining figures of the deceased and his wife.

Fig. 185   Museum: sarcophagus from the necropolis of Hierapolis.

Hall A

On the right is an Ionic capital coming from the Temple of Apollo and a figured capital with lions attacking bulls from the stoa-basilica in the Agora. The first niche contains some marble statues of divinities. Against the wall is the colossal statue of an emperor, perhaps Hadrian, of which the lower part of the body is preserved, with a kneeling barbarian at his feet, coming from the Temple of Apollo (fig. 121). There is also a headless female statue (fig. 124).

Second niche

A portrait head of a youth, from the theatre, datable to late antiquity, perhaps to the beginning of the fourth century, especially because of the deeply incised pupils.

Along the wall, past the second niche, is a statue found in the theatre, showing a female figure with a mantle, rendered according to schemes deriving from the school of Praxiteles, with a characteristic hairdo with rows of curls in front, datable to Flavian times (end of the first century AD).

Fig. 186
Museum: marble portrait head of the fourth century AD from the theatre.

Against the back wall

The statue of a priestess from *Laodicea*, with anatomic forms highlighted by the drapery knotted beneath her breasts, typical of the women dedicated to the Egyptian Goddess Isis, as are also the curls that drop onto the sides of the neck and the lunar crescent of the diadem. A Corinthian capital with the bust of an Erote supporting garlands, coming from the central structure of the stoa-basilica in the Agora of Hierapolis. Acroterial figure of a Triton from the theatre, with forms that recall the naked giants in the altar of Pergamum. Capital with sphinxes from the stoa-basilica in the Agora, on which may be observed the intense and pathetic expression of the face that is linked, as with the statue of Triton, to the Hellenistic sculptural tradition of Pergamum (fig.s 84-85).

Fig. 187   Museum: Triton from the scaenae frons of the theatre.

Second niche on the left

Here is the sarcophagus from the so-called Beautiful Tomb ("Tomba Bella") (see p. 86), reconstructed from various fragments found in the area around the base of the monument. In Byzantine times the *heroon* was smashed to pieces, and partially reused in the neighbouring walls and partly burned to produce lime. The sarcophagus represents one of the masterpieces of micro-Asiatic sculpture of Julio-Claudian times (first half of the first century AD). It imitates the form of a building with four angular columns sustaining the architrave and the double gabled roof which constitutes the lid of the sarcophagus (fig. 63). In the upper part of the wall are suspended garlands interrupted by *bucrania*, with rosettes in the upper spaces. Architectural decorations are achieved with great finesse, whilst the Gorgon's head in the tympanum is quite expressive.

Along the sides of the sarcophagus-sacellum are a series of elegantly draped figures. On the long right side is the principal figure seated upon a throne, surrounded by standing figures. His torso is naked, and his raised arm holds a sceptre, giving him a princely status reinforced by the ribbon decorating his head.

On the short side a naked youth is crowned by a figure, represented by a surviving hand, in front of a draped female figure (fig. 65). The long left side also shows an incoronation scene, probably representing the same individual, wrapped in a mantle, to whom the tomb was dedicated, whilst another female figure looks on (fig. 64).

The sarcophagus is set upon a sumptuous marble base, with a beautiful frieze of scrolls that includes flowers and fruit, above a cornice moulding with an Aeolic kyma, rows of astragals and

Fig. 188 Museum: relief from the area of the temple nymphaeum.

Fig. 189 Museum: head of Hadrian.

pearls, acanthus leaves and a scale motif. On all four sides acanthus sprays are organised in correspondence with the pilasters of the sarcophagus. It is easy to imagine the harmonious monumentality of this *heroon*, placed on a great base revetted with marble and contained within an aedicule with a canopy that contributed to emphasise the context of apotheosis of the important personality buried there, following an authentic Hellenistic tradition of Asia Minor that extended from the Mausoleum of *Halicarnassos* to the Roman example at Milas.

There are also ideological connections with monuments such as that of Zoilos in nearby *Aphrodisias* which is not much earlier (Augustan), where we find the same form of exaltation through the images that surround the protagonist who is shown being crowned by personifications of the *Polis* (the city) or *Timé* (honour).

Recent studies by R.R. Smith have shown that even the reliefs of Zoilos where placed on the four sides of a base that belonged to the heroon of the famous freeman of Augustus.

First niche on the left

Various Hellenistic funerary stelae with inscriptions, including a stele with the double-axe from the surrounding territory, dedicated to Apollo (Lairbenos), with the rows of his faithful on various registers, presented in schematic stylisation, each one with his name inscribed on the lower part of the relief.

In the centre of the hall are various marble sarcophagi. Two were found in the funerary enclosure of Flavius Zeuxis: that with erotes, garlands and Gorgon masks, each with a different expression, probably of local manufacture, and that of Maximilla with flutings and a central inscribed tablet. Another sarcophagus with garlands and portrait busts of a couple on the front is of Antonine date and was found in the church above the theatre (21).

The largest sarcophagus of Sidamara type was instead found in the cemetery of *Laodicea*. It dates to the first half of the third century AD and shows the couple reclining on the lid/funerary bed. The coffin bears a background of niches and columns, and on the front stand various people to either side of the deceased, who is seated, dressed as a philosopher, with beard and curly hair. On the back the virtue and heroism of the deceased is represented by a lion hunt in which the protagonist on horseback is slaying the beast with his lance.

Hall B

Glass showcases to the right

Prehistoric finds: small idols of the mother-goddess dating to the Copper Age or Chalcolithic (5000-3000 BC).

The finds from the systematic excavations carried out by the English team at the *höyük* (an artificial hill created by the superimposition of various settlements) of Beycesultan, located along the upper Meander valley, to the north-east of Hierapolis, towards Afyon, date to the Early, Middle and Late Bronze Age (3000-1200 BC).

The stratified remains of this site, comprising extensive palatial structures, are comparable in importance to those at Troy and witness the contacts of this part of western Anatolia with the Aegean world dominated by the Mycenean civilisation.

Fig. 191 Museum: red-slipped Roman pottery.

Fig. 190 Museum: terracotta figurine showing a female divinity with a child.

215

Fig. 192
Museum: moulds for relief-decorated Megarian ware type bowls.

Fig. 193
Museum: glass unguentaria from the cemeteries.

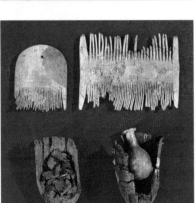

Fig. 194
Museum: wooden combs and containers for unguentaria from the cemeteries.

Fig. 195
Eucharistic mould with cross (middle) and eulogiai (small flasks for oil), from sacred Christian places. Fifth-sixth century AD.

Of note are the vases with incised geometric decoration with white inclusions, the grey pottery with burnished surfaces, the long nozzle jugs that clearly imitate metal prototypes in bronze or silver, pedestal vases, seals, stone objects and brazier stands, some of which are decorated.

Glass showcases against the back wall

Various objects coming from Archaic Greek and Hellenistic cemeteries in the territory: *oinochoe* (wine-jug) and two-handled cup in characteristic shiny "black glaze" pottery, dating to the third century BC. From Hierapolis come the red-slipped vases, the lamps and the personal items such as gold rings and earrings, a wooden comb, brooches, mirrors and necklaces with glass paste beads.

Glass showcases to the left

Various types of pottery, including Byzantine type glazed wares (eleventh to thirteenth centuries AD) with sgraffito decoration, found in one of the rooms of the Baths reused for housing in medieval times.

Glass showcases in the centre of the hall

Numismatic collection with coins dating from Archaic to Ottoman times. Note the Hellenistic silver examples of King Lysimachus, the gold coins from *Panticapeum* in Crimea with depictions of the Sphinx, a hoard of Roman Imperial times (second century AD) and a Byzantine gold tracheate (thin convex) coin. There is also an Egyptian basalt statue of a seated figure bearing an important Archaic Greek inscription.

Hall C

Here are the sculptures discovered during the excavations of the theatre of Hierapolis, dating to the beginning of the third century AD.

Right hand wall

Slabs with the Dionysian cortege: the chariot of Dionysius led by centaurs that play tympana and flutes, preceded by a Maenad and an Eros riding a panther; slabs with scenes from the Apollo cycle (see theatre 20, p. 161).

Back wall

Above a travertine block base is the frieze that lay above the central door to the theatre's *scaenae frons*. To the sides are two tondos with the busts of the Pergamene Kings Attalus and Eumenes, both bearded, with crowns on which are tied the fillets, symbols of power (fig. 198). The portraits are conventional and bear no links to the real physiognomy of the two sovereigns as they were represented at *Pergamum* in the second century BC. They were set in the stage of the theatre so as to emphasise the continuity of Roman Imperial power with the origins of Hierapolis and its links with the Kings of *Pergamum*.

The central frieze bears the scene of the celebration of the civic games by the Emperor Septimius Severus depicted as an enthroned Zeus in the centre of the composition, being crowned by a flying Nike (fig. 199). To his sides are his two sons, Caracalla to the left and Geta to the right, though the figure of Geta has been chiselled away by order of his fratricidal brother in an act of *damnatio memoriae* (the cancellation of portraits and inscriptions referring to a famous person or emperor who had fallen in disgrace). Next to Geta is the Empress Julia Domna with her head veiled in the act of performing a libation. The importance of the frieze also lies in the presence of a cornice with acanthus leaves and ovolos on which are inscribed the names of the figures who would not otherwise have been easily identifiable.

To the right of the Empress is a figure with a horn of plenty and a towered crown representing Tyche (the Good Fortune), whilst the seated figure with a helmet, lance and shield, which bears the image of a Sphinx, might represent the goddess Roma (at this point the inscription is missing).

The left hand side of the frieze is occupied by symbols of games. A large cylindrical metallic crown with decorative bosses sits on a table whilst, in front, lies a figure with a long beard representing the river-god of the city, called *Chrysorhoas* (from

Fig. 196
Museum, from the theatre: tympanum with the bust of Tyche with the horn of abundance.

Fig. 197 Museum, from the theatre: tympanum with the bust of Apollo and the double-axe.

Fig. 198 Museum, from the theatre: shield with the bust of the King of Pergamum, Eumenes.

Fig. 199   Museum, from the theatre: frieze showing the Imperial family (Septimius Severus, Julia Domna, Caracalla and Geta) in front of the games' crown.

Fig. 200   Museum, from the theatre: Severan period frieze with the scene of a sacrifice. To the right is Aion, time without end.

Fig. 201 Museum, from the theatre: frieze with the figure of the agonothetes, the organiser of the games.

Fig. 202 Museum, from the theatre: frieze with the figure of Demetra on the chariot.

Fig. 203
Museum, from the theatre: frieze showing a Dionysian cortege.

the golden currents) in coin inscriptions. Next to the crown a female figure lifts an object, perhaps the *agalma* (the votive statue) of Apollo Pythios, protector of the city. The inscription identifies her as the personification of Hierapolis. This is followed by the image of Agonothesia, the symbol of the organisation of the games. At her feet is the amphora from which were extracted the names of the athletes who would couple for the various games. On the far left, next to the tripod, stands the muscular figure of an athlete who is about to crown himself and who holds a palm, symbol of the winners of the athletic contests.

On the lateral blocks are depicted athletes of various types as well as other figures. The couple of figures on the left front face appear to be of particular importance: the *agonothetes* (the promoter and organiser of the contests) with a short chiton, a mantle wrapped around the body and a crown decorated with small busts (that represent the emperor and divinities), sign of the

Fig. 204
Museum, from the theatre: frieze showing centaurs that pull the chariot of Dionysus.

223

priesthood of the Imperial cult (fig. 201). In this figure, as in that of Septimius Severus and the Imperial family in the centre of the relief, the fattened facial features and the small mouth reveal a physiognomic intent and refer to an influential figure at Hierapolis, promoter of the games and holder of public offices. To the right, the veiled female figure may represent a priestess or the personification of the Boulé, the citizen assembly.

On the right block there are further figures and athletes that are taking part in the celebration of the games. To the side of the goddess Roma is another female figure with a short chiton, sword, helmet and lance, indicated in the inscription as *Andreia*, the personification of value and valour. She is followed by *Synodos*, the association of scenic artists, represented as a female figure with her hand on her head in the act of contemplating a theatrical mask. Wrapped in a large mantle is *Dadouchos*, the priestess carrying the torch. On the front right face of the block is a naked athlete being crowned by another figure wrapped in a large mantle.

The themes that are developed through images in this frieze, as in the cycles of Apollo and of Artemis (see pp. 161-181), make use of a complex network of literary and symbolic references. This is a typical language, non only of the figurative arts, in which the influence of the New Sophistry, the philosophical movement that profoundly oriented the cultural life of Asia Minor during the centuries of the Roman Empire, is to be seen.

In the centre of the hall towards the entrance

A winged sphinx and a capital with representations of the *venationes* (games of animal hunts, with a variety of beasts).

In the centre

Small pediments that formed part of the decoration of the *scaenae frons* with busts of divinities: Selene (Moon) with her lunar crescent; Apollo Lairbeinos with a mantle, his double-axe and a typical hairstyle, flanked by an oak-branch and a vine-branch (fig. 197); Tyche, the goddess of abundance, with the horn of plenty (fig. 196).

Fig. 206   Museum, from the theatre: fragments of the head of Leto.

Fig. 205
Museum, from the theatre: statue of Leto, mother of Apollo and Artemis.

Left wall towards the entrance

Blocks showing the rape of Proserpine, in which the powerful figure of Hades, god of the underworld, on a four-horse chariot driven by Eros, symbol of love, drags away the goddess. She extends her arms, terrified, whilst the *kalathos* that she held falls to earth. The reins of the fleeing horses are held by the figure of Hermes, with his *petasos* (wide-brimmed hat) and a caduceus in

Fig. 207
Museum, from the theatre: statue of Hades.

his hand (the stick with intertwined snakes, symbol of the divinity). The vigour of the nude god is accentuated by the open composition.

Within the niche

A headless marble statue of Apollo (on the base we may read *Kareios Apollon*). This is a unique illustration of the god invoked by the oracle. He has a chiton tied at his waist, decorated leggings and a himation that drops down from his shoulders and is fixed on his chest by a circular boss. Next to him is a statue of Artemis the huntress with her hair gathered on her head, a chiton with many folds and a double quiver crossed over her chest.

Left wall, towards the back

Slabs from the decoration of the podium of the *scaenae frons*, with the birth of Apollo, the Marsyas cycle, etc. (see pp. 161).

Fig. 208
Unfinished sculpture.

APPENDIX

How to consult the oracle of Apollo

Even the ancients, like today, were driven by the desire to know what the future held in store. For this reason, again like today, they interrogated fortune-tellers and prognosticators, or they went directly to consult their gods in the most famous sanctuaries such as Delphi or Dodone in mountainous Epirus. In Anatolia they went to interrogate Apollo at Claros and at Didyma, near Miletus. The gods replied through complicated rituals and manifestations that were interpreted, not always unambiguously, by the priests and female prophets.

At Hierapolis, like in other sanctuaries of Western Anatolia, the god expressed himself through alphabetic oracles. Two inscriptions have been found, dating to the second or third centuries AD, one in the enclosure of the Temple of Apollo, the other reused in the octagonal *martyrion* of St. Philip, that allow us to reconstruct the entire text. The beginning of each verse corresponds to each letter of the Greek alphabet. However, the oracle does not refer to Apollo of Delphi, but rather to a native divinity, Kareios, assimilated to Apollo by the Greeks. From the theatre comes a statue of this youthful divinity, who was linked to the underworld and dressed like the male divinities of Anatolia, such as Men, who was connected to the lunar cult.

It is easy to consult the oracle and you can do it by going to the grotto of the Plutonium. You must prepare 24 tickets, as many as the letters of the Greek alphabet, and mark each one with a separate letter. Then all you have to do is extract a ticket. In the following text you can find, in correspondence to the letter that you have chosen, the answer to your queries.

Alphabetic oracle of the Sanctuary of Apollo Kareios at Hierapolis:

Α [α]ὐτός σοι τελέσει καιρῷ θεὸς ὅσσα μεριμνᾷς.
(The god himself will sort out for you, in his own time, that for which you are anxious)

Β βουλαῖς ταῖς ἀγαθαῖς Τύχη πρέσβειρα παρέσται.
(The venerable Tyche will assist the good decisions)

Γ γειαρότης, ὥς φασι, δέχου κόλποισιν ἔχιδναν.
(Farmer, as they say, take a snake into your bosom)

Δ δείματα δεινὰ φοβοῦ, σκέπτου δὲ πρὶν ἤ σέ τι δρᾶσα[ι.]
(Fear the things that should be feared, reflect before doing anything)

Ε εὐάντητον ἔχων Νέμεσιν ἔργοις ἐπιθάρσε[ι.]
(As Nemesis is propitious, have faith in you actions)

Ι ζωῆς εἰσὶ χρόνοι· τί μάτην, ἄνθρωπε, μεριμν[ᾷς;]
(Life has its own times: why, man, are you needlessly anxious?)

Η ἡ Νέμεσις θνητοῖς Δίκη<ς> πλάστινγας ἀλεύε[ι.]
(Nemesis shakes the scales of justice for mortals)

Θ θαρραλέως τὴν πρᾶξιν ὑπόστα καὶ κατάπρα[ξον.]
(Resolutely take action and conclude it)

I   ἰσχὺν ἐργασίη<ς> δώσει κλυτότοξος Ἀπόλλων.

(Apollo who holds the glorious bow will give you strength in your feats)

K   κύμασιν μάχεσθαι χαλεπόν, ἀνάμεινον βρα[χύ.]

(It is difficult to combat the waves: bide your time)

Λ   λάμβανε, κ<οι>νωνεῖ καὶ προσδέχου λοιπὸν χαράν.

(Take, share and thus receive joy)

M   μάτην ἐπείγῃ μὴ τάχυν' οὐ συνφέρει.

(You are proceeding in vain, don't hurry, its pointless)

N   νυκτὸς ἀπὸ ζοφεῆς ἐφάνη ποτὲ φωσφόρος ἀκτή.

(From the tenebrous night once appeared a luminous ray)

Ξ   ξεῖνοι σύνβουλοί σ' ἐποδηγήσουσιν ἄμεινο[ν.]

(External advice will guide you better)

O   ὄμφαξ ἤν μείνῃς ἔσται καιροῖσι πεπείρο[ις.]

(Sour grapes, if you wait, will mature in their own time)

Π   πτηνοὺς καὶ κόρακας νωθεῖς προθέουσι χέλ[υες.]

(The slow tortoises precede the crows, even if they are winged)

P   ῥεύμασι μὴ πειρῶ πλώειν μόνος ἀντὶ φέρεσθ[αι.]

(Don't try, if you sail alone, to oppose the currents)

Σ   σώσει σ' ἀθανάτων βασιλεὺς χρησμοῖσι Κάρει[ος.]

(The King of the Immortals will save you with the oracles of Kareios)

T   τί σπεύδεις; δύνασαι μείνας ἱλαρώτερος ἐλθεῖν.

(Why hurry? If you wait you can go with greater happiness)

Υ ὕστερον οὐκ ἔσται τι, καὶ εἰ νῦν ἐστὶν ὕφοπτον.

(If there is still time, later there will be nothing suspect)

Φ φαύλους φεῦγε φίλους, πίστευε δὲ τοῖσιν ἀρίστοις·

(Escape from friends that are worth little and trust the best)

Χ χάρμα σοι ἀπροδίελπτον ἄγει θεὸς ὅς σε φυλάσσει.

(The god that looks after you will bring you an unexpected joy)

Ψ ψυχῆς ἐρχόμενον καὶ σώματος ἴσθι καθαρμόν.

(Know that purification of soul and body is arriving)

Ω ᾧ θεὸς εἵλαός ἐστι τύχην τροσένειμε Κάρειος.

(To whoever the god is favourable, Kareios concedes fortune)

GLOSSARY

apse	a typical element of Roman and Christian architecture, of semicircular or polygonal shape, usually at the end of a nave.
agones	athletic or musical games that took place in Greek cities.
agonothetes	organiser of games.
agora	the square of a Greek city (equivalent to the Latin *forum*), a place for meetings and market activities.
Amazonomachy	battle between the Greeks and the Amazons, a mythical society of warrior women that inhabited the Black Sea coast between the Paphlagonian mountains and the Pontic Alps.
analemma	the wall that in ancient Greek theatres served to contain the seats of the cavea.
anastilosis	reconstruction of ancient buildings through recomposition of original structures.
antefix	a painted ceramic decorative element that ends the roof tiles on the roofs of temples and other ancient buildings.
apotropaic	serving to distance evil influences.
apotheosis	elevation of a person from mortal to divine status.
arcosolium	tomb within a wall or surmounted by a niche.
attic	in architecture, the part above the cornice; it can consist of a wall, as in Roman triumphal arches, or in an upper storey with columns, pilasters and architraves.
bomòs	pedestal, altar; in cemetery inscriptions it indicates the basement upon which sarcophagi were placed.

Chalcolithic	the period that marks the passage between the late stone age (Neolithic) and the bronze age; in Anatolia it dates between 5.000 and 3.000 BC
calidarium	heated room in Roman baths.
caravanserai	in the East, an enclosure for the stopover of caravans formed of a large courtyard surrounded by buildings.
cavea	in the theatre, the area containing the seats of the audience, divided by the diazoma into an upper *(summa cavea)* and a lower *(ima cavea)* half.
chrismon	monogram that represents the name of Christ, formed of the letters *chi* and *rho*, with the function of symbolic invocation.
chtonic	subterranean; it refers to divinities linked to the Underworld such as Pluto.
cloaca	drain; underground channel that collects rainwater and liquid waste.
diazoma	corridor that divides, horizontally, the areas of the cavea in the ancient theatre.
Dike	Greek personification of Justice, daughter of Zeus and Themis (the deity of law and order).
epistyle	in ancient architecture, the architrave and blocks sitting upon the columns.
fornix	in architecture, the large opening crowned by an arch.
gymnasium	in ancient Greece the place where naked young men practised athletics; later a place for lessons, banquets and meetings.
Gorgon	in Greek mythology, the head of Medusa, of horrible aspect with serpents amidst the hair and capable of turning to stone whoever looks at her.
helix	each of the small volutes of the Corinthian capital.
heroon	small sanctuary or tomb dedicated to the cult of a hero.
hipostyle	a room which roof was supported by columns.

Hippodamean	referred to the urban layout of Hippodamus of Miletus, indicating a city plan based on right-angled axes.
hypocaust	a system used in Roman baths for heating rooms: hot air from a furnace was made to circulate beneath pavements supported by small brick piers *(suspensurae)*.
hypogeum	underground.
intrados	the visible interior surface of an arch or vault.
kalathos	in Greek, basket; part of the Corinthian capital.
katharsios	in Greek, purifier.
kyma	in classical architecture, the double-curved undulation of a moulding.
martyrion	a type of building in Christian architecture, usually with a central plan, in memory of a martyr.
Megarian ware	a class of Hellenistic pottery that takes its name from the city of Mègara; it is characterised by relief decoration produced through the use of a mould.
micro-Asiatic	from ancient Asia Minor, where micro translates into minor.
moulding	moulded part of an architectural feature.
monolithic	formed of a single stone block.
narthex	part of the Christian church reserved for catechumens (unbaptised Christians), composed of a vestibule in front of the church façade.
necropolis	area of a city used for burials, cemetery.
New Sophistry	Graeco-Roman cultural movement developed between the first and the fourth century A.D, particularly in Asia Minor, and based on rhetoric seen as the patrimony of moral truths.
nymphaeum	monumental fountain; in Roman times with sumptuous architectural decoration, statues and reliefs.
peribolos	in ancient architecture, a sacred enclosure around a temple.

peristyle — a colonnade that surrounds a courtyard; a colonnaded portico that surrounds a building.

personification — the representation of an abstract concept through the use of a human figure.

platèia — in ancient town planning, the main street, as opposed to the stenopòs, a secondary or side street.

Plutonium — at Hierapolis, the entrance to the underworld, identified next to the temple of Apollo.

postern — in fortifications, a small gate, sited away from the main entrances.

praefurnium — in ancient Roman baths, a space intended for heating water, located next to the *calidarium*.

protome — a common feature of ancient art, composed of the head of an animal or human figure.

pseudo-transept — false transept (the transversal nave that in churches with a Latin-cross plan is placed perpendicualr to the nave).

sarcophagus — from the Greek σαρκοφάγος, "which eats or consumes the flesh"; an urn of stone, marble or metal.

Seleucid — referred to the Seleucid dynasty that reigned in Syria and the East after the death of Alexander.

Seljuk — referred to the Turkish dynasty that settled in Asia Minor from the eleventh century.

stylobate — in Greek architecture, a row of blocks beneath the columns.

stoa — covered portico, consisting of a colonnade in front and a wall behind.

tholos — in Greek architecture, a circular building.

SELECT BIBLIOGRAPHY

Travellers and early explorations

L. DE LABORDE, *Voyage de l'Asie Mineure*, Paris 1838, pp. 81ff.

CH. TEXIER, *Description de l'Asie Mineure*, Paris 1839, pp. 35ff.

W.M. RAMSAY, *The Cities and Bishoprics of Phrygia*, Oxford 1897, pp. 84ff.

C. HUMANN, C. CICHORIUS, W. JUDEICH and F. WINTER, *Altertümer von Hierapolis*, in JDAI, Ergänz. 4, 1898.

General works and principal monuments

D. DE BERNARDI FERRERO, *Teatri classici in Asia Minore*, I, Rome 1966, pp. 57-76.

P. VERZONE, *L'urbanistica di Hierapolis di Frigia*, Turin 1972.

T. RITTI, *Fonti letterarie ed epigrafiche. Hierapolis*, Scavi e Ricerche, I, Rome 1985.

Hierapolis di Frigia. 1957-1987, exhibition catalogue, Milan 1987.

D. DE BERNARDI FERRERO, *Hierapolis, in Scavi archeologici italiani in Turchia*, Venice 1993.

F. D'ANDRIA-F. SILVESTRELLI (eds.), *Ricerche archeologiche turche nelle valle del Lykos* (in Italian and Turkish), Galatina 2000.

F. D'ANDRIA, *Hierapolis of Phrygia: Its Evolution in Hellenistic and Roman Times*, in D. PARRISH (ed.), *Urbanism in Western Asia Minor*, JRA, Suppl. no. 45, 2001, pp. 96-115.

The Christian city

P. VERZONE, *Le chiese di Hierapolis*, in *Cahiers archéol.*, 8, 1956, pp. 37ff.

P. VERZONE, *Il Martyrium ottagono a Hierapolis di Frigia*, in *Palladio*, n.s. 10, 1960, pp. 1ff.

Sculpture

F. D'ANDRIA and T. RITTI, *Le sculture del teatro. Hierapolis, Scavi e Ricerche, II, Rome 1985*, with *Note sulla decorazione architettonica della fronte scena del teatro di Hierapolis*, by D. DE BERNARDI FERRERO, pp. xix-xxviii.

G. BEJOR, *Le Statue. Hierapolis, Scavi e Ricerche*, III, Rome 1991.

ILLUSTRATIONS

All photographs and plans are from the archives of the Italian Archaeological Mission in Hierapolis.

F. Baratti	general plan of Hierapolis, p. 44
F. Basile	fig.s 62, 122, 123, 147a-b, 164, 190, 191, 193, 194, 199, 200
G. Bejor	fig. 207
G. Comollo	fig.s 133, 136
F. D'Andria	fig.s 6, 11, 14, 25, 26, 27, 28, 34, 35, 40, 41, 42, 45, 48, 51, 52, 54, 57, 59, 61, 66, 67, 68, 69, 70, 71, 72,73, 75, 79, 80, 82, 83, 84, 85, 86, 87, 89, 90, 91, 93, 96, 101, 102, 103, 104, 105, 106, 109, 111, 113, 116, 117, 118, 119, 120,, 121, 124, 125, 126, 127, 128, 129, 132, 134, 135, 137, 138, 139, 140, 141, 143, 148, 149, 152, 153, 154, 155, 156, 162, 163, 165, 167, 171, 173, 175, 176, 177, 178, 179, 180, 181, 182, 183, 184, 185, 186, 187, 188, 189, 192, 196, 197, 198, 201, 202, 203, 204, 205, 206, 208
D. De Bernardi Ferrero	fig.s 19, 20, 31, 115
De Laborde 1838	fig.s 12, 16
J. Devreker	fig.s 22, 23, 24, 55, 81
M.A. Döğenci	fig.s 43, 63, 65, 77, 99a-b, 108, 110
F. Ghio - L. Campagna	fig. 100
J. Cl. Golvin	pp. 46-47
N. Gullino	fig. 157

O. Henry	fig. 2
Hierapolis 1987	fig.s 36, 112, 114, 130, 160, 168, 174
Kachler	fig. 15
R. Mondazzi	fig.s 142a-b, 150a-b
P. Perfido	fig. 58
Quaresima	fig.s 144, 145, 146, 151
R. Rachini	fig.s 53, 60, 74, 76, 78, 94
M.P. Rossignani	fig. 78
F. Sergi	fig. 97
M. Vantaggiato	fig.s 3, 4, 5, 7, 8, 9, 10, 13, 17, 18, 21, 29, 30, 32, 33, 37, 38, 44, 46, 47, 49, 50, 56, 92, 95, 98, 107, 131, 158, 159, 169, 172
P. Verzone	fig.s 39, 161

Francesco D'Andria

Born at Laterza (Taranto, Italy) in 1943, Francesco D'Andria studied at the Catholic University of Milan, specialising in classical archaeology. After a brief period as Inspector of Archaeology at the Superintendency of Molise, he now holds the chair in Greek and Roman Archaeology and Art history at the University of Lecce, where he also directs the Post-graduate School of Archaeology. He is a member of the Italian National Council for Cultural Heritage. He is also a correspondent of the *Deutsches Archaeologisches Institut* of Berlin and member of the Scientific Committee of the journal *Archeo*. Research on the Messapian and other Adriatic cultures in antiquity have allowed him to develop strong links between the University of Lecce and research institutes in Yugoslavia, Greece and Albania. For the University of Lecce, and in collaboration with the Ecole Française a Rome and the Scuola Normale di Pisa, he also directs excavations at the sites of Oria, Otranto, Cavallino and Vaste, in Apulia (southern Italy), and is responsible for their publication in a series edited by the University. He has taken part in various seasons of excavations at Luni, in Magna Graecia (Metaponto, Sibari) and, in the Mediterranean, on Malta, Cyprus and in Turkey. At Segesta, in Sicily, he co-ordinates a research project on the ancient theatre, in collaboration with the Archaeological Superintendency of Trapani, the Scuola Normale of Pisa and Turin Polytechnic. He is director of the Italian Archaeological Mission in Hierapolis.

His publications include: *The Roman bronzes of Veleia* (1970); *Roman Apulia* (1979); *The sculpture of the Theatre at Hierapolis in Phrygia* (1985); *Computers and Classical Archaeology* (ed.), (1986); *Archaeology of the Messapians* (1990).